Chilterns
40 favourite Walks

published by
pocket mountains ltd
The Old Church, Moffat, DG10 9HB
pocketmountains.com

ISBN: 978-1-907025-59-4

Printed in Poland

Introduction

The Chiltern Hills are widely regarded as one of Britain's finest landscapes, famous for rolling chalk hills, rich grassland, beechwoods, picturesque villages and winding lanes. For the walker, it is close to heaven with a seemingly endless network of public footpaths, some of which have been in use for thousands of years. They lead through fields and woods, into villages and over farmland, past ancient hamlets and stately homes, up steep hillsides, or down to the valley floor. Depending on the season, your day will be filled with golden beech trees, red kites, bluebells and butterflies. Brick and flint houses line the roadsides, thatched cottages and Norman churches lie around the corner – all close to London, yet far from the crowds. What's more, this being an affluent corner of England you are never too far from a characterful pub or a tearoom to reward yourself for a route well followed. A walk in the Chilterns? Go on. You'll love it.

The Chilterns

The Chilterns are easier to describe than to define. While the boundaries might be up for discussion, their appeal is not: the Chilterns are recognised as one of the UK's Areas of Outstanding Natural Beauty (AONB), beginning in the south at Goring-on-Thames and running northeast for 80km through Oxfordshire, Buckinghamshire, Berkshire, Hertfordshire and into Bedfordshire. They are most clearly defined along the northwestern edge by the steep chalk escarpment, roughly bounded by the M4 motorway in the south, the M1 in the north and the M25 to the east, where they slope down into the Thames Basin. London is close – indeed Chesham and Amersham are stops on the London Underground's Metropolitan Line. The Saxons, who incidentally gave the area its name (*Chilt* is the Anglo-Saxon term for 'Chalk'), regarded the hills as godforsaken and a place where 'no-one in their right minds would want to settle'. These days, there is no shortage of people who would like to live in the hills, although relatively few can afford to do so. The rich and famous enjoy riverside properties at Goring-on-Thames, or convert venerable farmsteads into desirable residences. Major towns have grown around the fringes, such as Dunstable, Luton, High Wycombe and Hemel Hempstead.

In spite of the pressures of modern development and urban expansion, the Chilterns remain predominantly rural, with farmland still covering around 60 percent of the landscape, and more than 20 percent given over to woodland. The chalk rock, a pure white limestone, has shaped the history as well as formed the hills. Stone Age people lived in the Chilterns, hunting and gathering, making good use of the plentiful flint for tools. When they began to settle, trees were cleared for crops, and the grassy downland, for which the Chilterns are known today, began to appear. The Romans built roads and villas, the Saxons established villages and field systems, and the Normans created churches which have survived for a thousand years. Many of the farms and hamlets are mentioned in the Domesday Book. The *Magna Carta* was signed in Dunstable and, in the Civil War, Royalist troops were rallied in a hostelry which still welcomes guests to this day. Walkers in the Chilterns will see Iron Age hillforts, Bronze Age burial mounds, medieval deer parks, 18th-century saw pits, 19th-century windmills and trenches from the First World War. The history – ancient and modern – reflects the layers of toil and habitation which have shaped the landscape and made the Chilterns quite different, and utterly enthralling.

Walking in the Chilterns

Three cheers for the Chiltern Society! Its staff and volunteers do a marvellous job of looking after the Rights of Way. They negotiate with landowners, erect signposts, clear nettles, reinforce banking, paint waymarkers – everything possible to help us enjoy the countryside without conflicting with those who live and work in it. There is a vigorous programme of stile replacement in progress which means you are more likely to pass through a kissing gate these days than climb a stile.

Almost invariably footpaths are clearly signposted, and many are waymarked, either by arrows on posts or painted in white on the bark of trees. It is important to keep to the established routes and not to stray onto private land. Always respect signs which keep you on the proper route, even though some might be bluntly worded.

People have been walking the lanes and paths of the Chiltern Hills for thousands of years. The Icknield Way, which runs along the Chiltern escarpment, is said to be the oldest road in Britain, although the exact course changed according to the season and conditions. Even in Saxon times, the travellers and drovers switched routes when wet weather and the heavy clay soil combined to make the path muddy and impassable. In that respect little has changed. Chiltern paths can be very muddy, especially when they are shared with horses and cyclists. Even in the height of summer, you will find tracks churned by hooves and wheels. It is often possible to find a way round the worst sections, but sometimes there is no alternative but to tackle the mud head on. On flat ground this is merely inconvenient, but on slopes it can be tricky and even dangerous. Some walks include very steep inclines and rarely are they completely flat, so good walking boots or shoes are essential.

In spite of the mud warnings, water is generally rather absent from the Chiltern countryside. Outside the villages, ponds are quite unusual and most of the valleys are dry, without a river or stream flowing along the bottom. Some of the routes are demanding and, in hot weather, dehydration is always a danger. Do carry drinking water with you. Be wary of walking in short trousers – nettles grow faster than the volunteers can beat them back. The usual rules apply to gates – leave them as you find them – and to dogs – keep them under control and away from livestock and always clean up after them. The paths and byways of the Chilterns are refreshingly litter free so make sure you take your litter home with you. Finally, always make sure that someone knows your intended route and what time you are expected back.

Wildlife and nature

Wherever you go in the Chiltern countryside, it's pretty much guaranteed that if you look to the skies you'll see a red kite. Driven to extinction by the late 19th century, they were re-introduced at the end of the 20th century and this has been so successful that red kites from the Chilterns have been used to rebuild colonies in other parts of the country.

They float over countryside brimming with life and colour. The grassland is a varied palette of wildflowers in spring and summer. Butterflies thrive in the chalk downs with equally colourful names like the Orange Tip, the Chalk Hill Blue and the Purple Hairstreak.

The woods, lime green in spring and golden in the autumn, are filled with birdsong. Young trees reach for the sky alongside pollarded oak, coppiced beech and ancient chestnut. Muntjac and fallow deer can often be spotted grazing beneath the canopy. The area boasts many nature reserves, often run by local groups and all worth a visit if you pass.

Getting around

As most of the major towns in the Chilterns have train stations and many of the villages are served by buses, it is theoretically possible to travel to many of the walks in this guide using public transport, although it does take a bit of planning. There is no denying that it is a lot easier by car. Parking suggestions are given for each walk, some of which involve a modest daily charge, although this volume tries to steer you towards free parking where it is available. If you have to park at the roadside, take care not to block access or passing places. Some car parks have height restricting barriers, usually set at around 1.8m.

Using this guide

All of the walks in this guide end where they begin (although one requires a short hop on the London Underground), so you won't have to worry about how to get back to your car. Each walk is prefaced with information to help plan your outing. The duration is based on the length of time it took the authors to walk the route, averaging about 3.5km per hour. It does not allow for stopping to enjoy the view, lingering over a picnic or exploring the various attractions and sights along the way, so make sure you build in plenty of time for these activities.

Postcodes, which are included to guide you towards the start of each walk, are approximate only and get you as near as SatNav technology can manage to the start. Sketch maps are for information rather than navigation. In England, Rights of Way are shown on Ordnance Survey maps and it is a good idea to carry the relevant OS map during the walk. Any compass directions are approximate, and all lefts and rights are given according to the direction of travel.

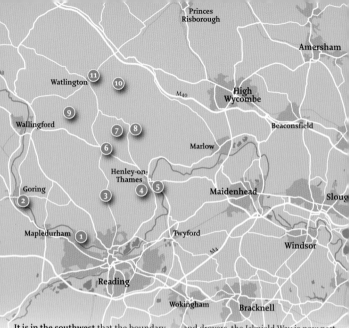

It is in the southwest that the boundary of the Chilterns is, arguably, most easily defined. Here, by common consent and official designation, the River Thames separates the Chilterns from the surrounding countryside, just as it marked the ancient border between Wessex and Mercia, and Oxfordshire and Berkshire today.

At Goring, travellers in Neolithic times – some 4000 years ago – crossed the river on what we now call the Icknield Way, widely regarded as England's oldest road. In truth, it was never a 'road', more a loosely woven series of parallel tracks along and beside the escarpment. Historically a trading route for travellers and drovers, the Icknield Way is now part of a network of long-range paths which help make the Chilterns such terrific walking country.

From Goring, the Thames skirts the southern fringes of the Chilterns to Henley, famous for its annual regatta, but one of the jewels of the Chilterns even without its riverside location.

Moving northwest from Henley through some of the prettiest countryside in England, across meadows and commons, through villages and valleys, you come to Watlington Hill. Here the Oxfordshire Chilterns have their northern boundary, although the view from the summit seems to go on forever.

The South

Mapledurham

Distance **4km** Time **1 hour 30**
Terrain **tracks and paths**
Map **OS Explorer 171**
Access **no public transport to the start**

When the producers of the 1976 film
The Eagle Has Landed, starring Michael
Caine, were looking for an unspoilt,
typically English village, they chose
Mapledurham. Even today, it seems
untouched by the passage of time, with
its Elizabethan manor, brick and flint
church and historic mill. Just across the
river from the urban sprawl of Reading,
the lack of a bridge between the two
has spared Mapledurham from the
pressures which have changed so many
Chiltern communities.

There is a small car park by the church
at Mapledurham which walkers are
allowed to use, by kind permission of the
landowner (RG4 7TR). Before setting off

up the village street, have a look at the
Church of St Margaret with its tombs,
medieval stained glass and ancient font.
Unless you are lucky enough to find your
visit coincides with one of the days when
the mill is open to the public, the railings
opposite the church gate are as close as
you can get to the last working mill on
the River Thames.

With the car park on your right, walk up
the village street until you can turn right
after the last house, with a postbox in the
garden wall. This takes you along a
concrete track, officially a bridleway, past
the gardens of the house and out across
the farmland. The River Thames is across
the fields to your right, although you
cannot see it at this point.

Further along you get a good view of
the front of Mapledurham House, with its
impressive red-brick exterior. Completed
in the late 16th century by Sir Richard

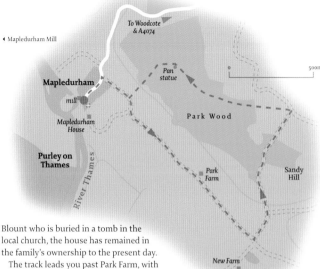

◄ Mapledurham Mill

Blount who is buried in a tomb in the local church, the house has remained in the family's ownership to the present day.

The track leads you past Park Farm, with its 400-year-old barn close to the road. Some 500m beyond, turn left at a road junction by a house to follow the track uphill. Keep left at the fork with a grain store to your right and watch for the evidence that someone rode a horse this way before the concrete was set!

As the track carries on uphill, it passes through a cutting in the woods and eventually emerges onto open farmland at the top. Take the gate into a field on your left, opposite the track to Rose Farm. The field may be cultivated, but a path heads directly over it to enter the woods by a marker post. The path then runs through the trees, turning downhill and crossing a grass track on the way.

Look out for primroses in the spring and keep a keen eye out for a statue of Pan, mounted high on a brick plinth just to the left of the path. Obscured by two huge yew trees and easy to miss, it once looked down over Mapledurham House. It is said to have been instigated by the famous 18th-century poet Alexander Pope, a frequent visitor to the house who was courting two sisters who lived there. He professed to be in love with each of them on alternate days.

From the statue, follow the path downhill and out of the woods via a gate into the field with the house straight ahead. Cross the field and turn right onto the concrete track back to the village.

9

Goring and Hartslock Reserve

Distance **6.5km** Time **2 hours**
Terrain **lanes and paths; one steep climb**
Map **OS Explorer 171** Access **buses and trains to Goring & Streatley Railway Station**

Goring sits on the intersection of three ancient transport routes and, in Saxon times, was an important crossing point over the Thames between Streatley in Wessex and Goring in Mercia. The river once marked the border between the kingdoms; now it forms the boundary between Berkshire and Oxfordshire. This walk combines town, country and the banks of England's most famous river.

Public parking in Goring is restricted mainly to the pay and display areas in the centre of town or to the station on Gatehampton Road (RG8 0ES).

Leaving the railway station, head right and follow the road out of the town. Keep left at the first fork and stay on the road until it bends uphill to the left. Go right here onto a track leading into the trees to the entrance to the Hartslock Reserve on your right. Across the field are two gates. Go through the one on the left to reach a flight of steps taking you up the steep hillside. The grassland by your right hand is filled with orchids and access is restricted at certain times of year when the plants need to recover. At the top of the hill there are wonderful views out over the River Thames.

Return to the bottom of the hill, either by keeping to the right-hand edge of the orchid-rich grassland if access is allowed or, if not, using the steps you used to come up. Whichever route you take, turn left at the bottom and walk towards the

river with the fence by your left hand. Go through a gate and turn right onto the Thames Path with the river on your left. After 500m, the path starts to bend away from the river. Take the cinder footpath that goes left, over a footbridge back to the water's edge, where you turn right to stay on the riverbank.

There may be cattle in the field after you pass under a railway bridge, but the path stays close to the water's edge with views of the impressive houses on both banks of the river – Goring on this side and Streatley on the other.

Soon the path opens out to become a tarmac walkway as you near the lock and roadbridge. This has been a river crossing since prehistoric times: the Icknield Way crossed here and, with the river being comparatively shallow at this point, the Romans chose to build a causeway. It was not bridged until 1837.

Immediately before the bridge, leave the footpath by turning right to pass the Old Mill on the way to the High Street. A mill has stood on this spot since Norman times, although the present building dates only from the 1920s.

Follow the High Street through the centre of town to the railway bridge. Cross over the railway and turn right to return to the station.

◀ A view of the Thames from Hartslock Hill

Rotherfield Peppard

Distance 8km **Time** 2 hours 30
Terrain paths, bridleways with some
short sections on the roadside
Map OS Explorer 171 **Access** buses from
Henley to Rotherfield Peppard

The little village of Rotherfield Peppard –
known locally as Peppard – lies just over
6km west of Henley. It gets its name
from the old English words for cattle
(*hryther*) and land (*feld*), combined with
the Pipard family who owned the land in
Norman times. Built round a green, it
makes a good start point for this walk
into the Oxfordshire countryside.

There are parking spaces on the green in
Peppard, across from the Red Lion (RG9
5LB). With the pub behind you, head out
to the B481, cross this and then fork right
onto Church Lane to walk with the green
to your right. Follow it past the school
and along to the 13th-century church.

Where the lane ends 50m beyond the
cemetery, take the footpath which sets off
to the left. Cross between fences to a gate
into young trees.

For the next 500m, the path runs
through woods between the fairways of
Greys Green Golf Course. Ignore any
paths that cross and, although you should
be safe in the woods, keep a wary eye out
for errant golf balls. Follow the path as it
leads through a gate, and turn left when
you join a lane by a cottage. After 150m,
cross a track onto the path behind a metal
gate to walk up between straggly hedging.

The field of young trees to your right is
Henley Woodland Burial Ground. Ignore
the gate which leads onto it, and follow
the path as it swings left round the corner

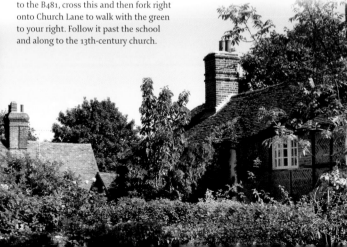

of the golf course.
It is pretty straight for the next 1km, as you cross a track and go through a gate to reach a road. Turn right and walk carefully along the verge for 250m until you see a cricket pitch on the other side. Cross over and leave the road immediately before the pitch to follow a driveway as it bends left. Pass through two gates ahead and enter the wood – ignoring any paths into the field on your left.

Forking left in the trees, the path leads you out along the edge of the fields. It will bring you through several gates to Shepherd's Green. Turn left on the public road for a few steps, then go right to walk up a gravel access road. Aim for the corner of the green where the path resumes in the trees. Go left in the field, keeping the fence close, to reach a gate. Bear slightly right across the next field and into the corner of woods.

The path leads through the trees, out across a field and into Padnell's Wood. Turn left at a T-junction in the trees and follow this path to the B481. Turn left and immediately bear left again into Satwell.

Follow the road for 175m, taking the first turning on the right to rejoin the main road. Cross with care and take the path which leads between houses and into woods. Go left at a fork and follow the path out of the trees, along the edge of a field and back into trees again.

When you come to a lane, cross over and continue in the same general direction until you come to a small clearing. Turn left and head uphill on a narrow path winding through the woods, ignoring any paths to your right until you meet the road again. Turn right and then left to walk across the common back to the Red Lion.

Henley to Rotherfield Greys

Distance **6.2km** **Time** **2 hours**
Terrain **footpaths and some public roads**
Map OS Explorer 171 **Access** **the Henley-on-Thames circular bus route stops at Deanfield Road, 300m from the start**

Rotherfield means 'cattle lands' in Old English and, in 1086, the Domesday Book recorded the owner as a Norman knight called De Greye. There are still some cattle in the fields here, along with many magnificent horse chestnut trees – not forgetting a direct link back to the days of the highwayman.

Park at the roadside in Tilebarn Close (RG9 1US) or Deanfield Road. The path begins to the right of the field gate just before the Henley College car park in Tilebarn Close. After 400m, by woodland planted to support a Sue Ryder hospice, you will cross a footpath called Pack and Prime Lane. The name harks back to the days when highway robbery was a constant threat to travellers. It was around here that the London to Oxford coach would stop to 'pack and prime' their guns in case of trouble.

Cross the lane to walk up the valley towards Lower Hernes, passing through a copse of horse chestnut trees below the house. Go straight ahead up a farm track (or the path beside it). Cross a track and walk on up the valley until you reach the end of an avenue of chestnut trees to your left. Look for a stile in the fence ahead of you and walk along the left side of the field to a farm gate and a stile, crossing this into the next field. Soon after, climb the stile on your left and walk up the side of the valley with a fence at your left hand. At the top, aim for the church to reach a road.

Turn right if you are in need of some refreshment – the Maltsters Arms is just

◀ A field near Rotherfield Greys

along the road – or go left to continue the walk. You will pass Pear Tree Cottages on your right. Two restorations have made it hard to believe this row of houses has been here for more than 500 years.

The next stretch involves walking along the roadside for about 300m. Follow it past the entrance to the Woodland Burial Ground until it bends to the left. The footpath continues straight ahead, across a field towards Cowfields Farm. Go past the gates and down a track with woodland on your right. With a left and right turn, the track will take you back to the road.

Turn right along a wide verge to

Highlands Lane. Cross the road onto the private drive to Hernes Estate, where a footpath heads diagonally across a field towards the right-hand end of the row of houses. A path between gardens brings you into a housing estate.

Cross the road ahead of you and go right to follow Nicholas Road down to a T-junction. Turn left to pass the entrance to Chiltern Close, and then walk up Two Tree Hill on the right-hand pavement. Where the road bends left, go straight ahead onto a footpath which leads you downhill into Tilebarn Lane. Go left to pick up the path again. It leads behind houses back to Tilebarn Close.

Pindars
Wood

Lower
Hernes

**Rotherfield
Greys**

Hernes ■

**Henley-on-
Thames**

Cowfields ■
Farm

Highlands
Farm

0   1km

Hambleden Lock from Henley

Distance **8km** Time **2 hours 30**
Terrain **towpath, tracks and paths**
Map **OS Explorer 171** Access **Henley is well
served by trains and buses; a summer
boat service also operates from Reading
and Marlow**

*It is not possible to do this walk during the
Regatta and Arts Festival which generally takes
place during the first two weeks in July.*

**Henley-on-Thames is one of those towns
which everyone should visit at some
point. It is brimming with buildings of
architectural interest and historical
significance, and is packed with
independent shops, quirky cafés and
venerable pubs. All this just a few steps
from one of the most famous rivers in the
world. The towpath is beside the course of
the world's best known rowing regatta.**

There are several pay and display car
parks in Henley, including one beside the
River and Rowing Museum on Mill
Meadows where the walk begins (RG9 1BF).

Head along the towpath with the river to
your right. Cross Henley Bridge, taking the
first turning on the left to walk back down
to the river. Turn right to put the river on
your left side.

This first stretch is the epicentre of the
rowing regatta, held over five days each
summer. Tents, grandstands, restaurants
and bars are set up here for an event which
is as much about the social occasion as the
sporting event. Once the regatta has
ended, a music and arts festival takes over
the facilities.

With Henley across the water, set off
along the towpath. The next 3.5km is
simply a matter of following the river,

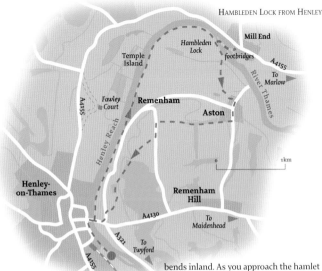

enjoying the ambience without worrying about directions. The river is pretty straight from Henley Bridge to Temple Island, where the regatta races start. The folly on the island was built in 1771 as a summerhouse for Fawley Court, the mansion on the opposite bank, which is linked by a wide channel to the Thames.

As the river bends right, look out for another large mansion, this one white, on the opposing bank. It was built for William Henry Smith who founded the chain of newsagents which still bears his name. At Hambleden Lock there is an exciting detour over the Thames on a walkway, allowing a good view of the weir and Hambleden Mill, now converted into flats.

To continue the walk, leave the lock to your left and follow the surfaced road as it bends inland. As you approach the hamlet of Aston, look for a path leading left onto Ferry Lane. Turn right on the lane, past the Flower Pot pub and on up the single-track road, leaving the pub car park to your right.

Just after the brick walls of an old bridge, take a path on the right along the side of a field. Follow the path for the next 1.25km as it becomes a track before it meets a lane.

Go left for 220m, then step through the gap in the right-hand hedge onto a footpath across a field, making for Remenham Wood. Follow the path through the woods and across the corner of a field before going back into woodland.

The path now leads through trees and across parkland to Remenham Lane. Turn left and walk round, past the Little Angel pub, to the main road. A right turn here will take you back over Henley Bridge for the towpath to the museum.

Nettlebed and the Berrick Trench

Distance **6km** Time **2 hours**
Terrain **woodland paths and tracks**
Map **OS Explorer 171** Access **buses from Henley and Wallingford to Nettlebed**

Starting from Nettlebed Bottle Kiln – one of the most recognisable buildings in the area – and visiting a secluded nature reserve and a Site of Special Scientific Interest, this is a typical Chilterns walk with splendid scenery, magical beech woodlands and rolling fertile farmland.

The A4130 rumbles through this picturesque village, and the shops which once lined the High Street have been largely driven away. It is easy to imagine how it looked in the days of coaches and horses. At the eastern end of the High Street, park at the roadside on the green close to the kiln, evidence of Nettlebed's once thriving brick industry (RG9 5BA).

This was one of several bottle kilns in the village in the 18th century. Today it is the only surviving example in the country. The bricks it produced were renowned for their strength and you can see them in use along the High Street.

Set off with the green to your right, passing Chapel Lane, and follow the road. Go left at the fork towards Magpies and walk along an avenue of trees to the entrance to Soundess House. It is said that Charles II sent his mistress Nell Gwyn to Soundess to escape the plague in London.

A track continues ahead into the trees, passing an information board about the Warburg Nature Reserve. It joins another track as you head down the slope and out

18

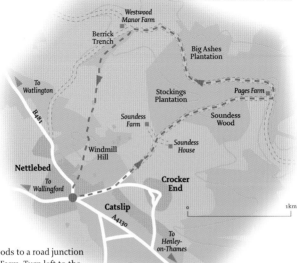

of the woods to a road junction by Pages Farm. Turn left to the Warburg Nature Reserve Visitor Centre 150m along the road.

Stay on the track between the visitor centre and car park to walk through the woods for over 1km. It gradually bends right until you are walking between hedges and fields. Go left at a farm track which leads along the valley floor towards Westwood Manor Farm. Turn left before the trees, heading up the side of a field and into the woods.

This is the Berrick Trench. The 'trench' is actually a long mound and has been designated as a Site of Special Scientific Interest, not least because of the variety of shrubs that grow here. Among the trees, you can find shrubs such as honeysuckle, goat willow, holly, buckthorn, spindle, guelder rose, spurge-

laurel, wych elm and old man's beard.

Follow the path up to a gate. Go across the field, heading to the left of the house in the distance. Pass an ornamental pond as you keep to the left edge of private grounds – a pleasant change not to be hidden away behind a fence – to join a track in front of the house.

Walk up the track until it bends right; at this point you head left. A white arrow on a tree will direct you. The arrows guide you up through the woods, branching left at a fork to eventually emerge from the trees with a steel fence on your left. Turn right onto the track and follow it down the slope to the road junction. Turn left and Nettlebed High Street is 120m along the road.

Maidensgrove to College Wood

Distance 10km Time 3 hours 30
Terrain grassland, woodland paths and
tracks Map **OS Explorer 171**
Access no public transport to the start

There can surely be no finer expanse
of common grassland in England than
Russell's Water and Maidensgrove
Common. Almost 2km from end to end
and mown once a year for hay, it makes for
a glorious beginning to this exploration of
the Chiltern countryside.

The common is roughly 7km north of
Henley and is most easily reached via
Stonor by the road at Maidensgrove (RG9
6EX). Set off across the grassland, with the
road to your left.

In the Second World War the common
was cultivated to grow food, but since
then it has been left to grass. Either follow
the path or, if the grass is young, choose
your own route, keeping generally to the
left side of the common. Cross a couple of
tracks and make your way to the top

corner, where the trees converge.

Take the path into the woods with a
white arrow on a tree for guidance, and
walk down the hill to a road. Cross over
and take the path leading up the slope,
turning right when you join another path.
Keep an eye out for muntjac deer as you
go, and cross any tracks as they appear.

You will drop into a shallow valley,
crossing a path at the bottom, and climb
up the other side. Follow the white arrows
on trees, often with the Chiltern Way
initials beside them.

Soon you cross a wide track and arrive
at a junction with paths heading in all
directions. Take the path between a white
arrow and blue marker and follow it
through the woodland to a track running
through a break in the trees. The path
continues on the other side of the
clearing, slightly to the left and indicated
by 'CW' painted beside an arrow on a tree.

It's a climb up through College Wood
now, over a stile, through a field to a

◄ Approaching Turville Park Farm

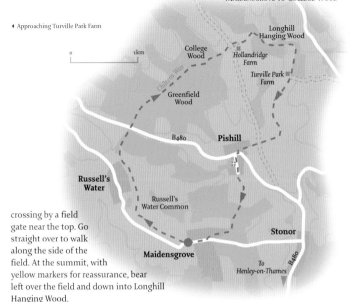

Longhill
Hanging Wood

College
Wood

Hollandridge
Farm

Turville Park
Farm

Greenfield
Wood

Chiltern Way

B480   Pishill

Russell's
Water

Russell's
Water Common

Stonor

0   1km

Maidensgrove   To
Henley-on-Thames   B480

crossing by a field gate near the top. Go straight over to walk along the side of the field. At the summit, with yellow markers for reassurance, bear left over the field and down into Longhill Hanging Wood.

Where the paths cross at the valley bottom, leave the Chiltern Way and bear right along a wide path. This will lead you out of the woods into farmland, curving to pass Turville Park Farm on your right.

Walk on down the valley to follow the grassy track on the left side of a field. Soon the track cuts through the hedge so the hedge is now on your right. Some 100m further on, turn right at the break in the hedge beside a tin hayshed and walk up the hillside, with the hedge – and a delightful view – to your left.

Cross a road, and follow the path down to a track. Turn left and walk a few steps before turning right on the road into

Pishill (pronounced like 'official') village.

Turn left after 30m into Church Hill. Go past the church and, when the road bends right, fork left to a wooden gate. Ignore the path heading right and go into the field ahead, following the left edge down to the corner. Cross a track and take the path which bears slightly right into the woods. White arrows guide you uphill.

Fork right as houses start to appear through the trees. Walk along a shingle drive, past the gable of a flint house on the left, onto a lane. After 250m, beyond a rather gloomy pond on the right, go right to step onto the common and return to the start.

Stonor Park

Distance 5.5km **Time** 2 hours
Terrain woodland paths, starting with a
pretty steep one, and a section of quiet
country road **Map** OS Explorer 171
Access no public transport to the start

The gates around Stonor Park are almost
2m high, with fences to match on either
side. That's because the house sits in a
deer park with around 150 fallow deer,
continuing a herd which has been in the
woods at Stonor since medieval times –
almost as long as the Stonor family has
lived in the house. After a steep climb out
of the village, the rest is level ground or
downhill, with wonderful views of the
house, grounds and, most likely, the deer.

Although no buses operate to Stonor
these days, there is a good-sized parking
area just opposite the bus shelter, by the
magnificent tile and timber barn at Upper
Assendon Farm (RG9 6HB). It is just as you
enter the village from the south.

Facing the farm buildings, look to your
right where a path sets off over a stile and
up the side of a field. For the first 500m, it
is all uphill, and pretty steep. At the top of
the field, the path climbs into Almshill
Wood, where white arrows painted on the
beech trees will guide you up the hillside.

As the path becomes less steep near the
top, it joins a track. Go left to continue up
the slope, following the white arrows that
lead you through to Cockslease Farm, with
sheds to your left and the house to the
right. Pass through a gate and head left
along the track to the public road.

Turn left along the quiet lane with fields,
hedges and woods for company, leaving
this to branch left at a signpost for
Southend after 1km. Follow this lane until it
is crossed by a track after 800m. Here, turn
left beside a pair of brick and flint cottages.
Pausing momentarily to admire the
intricate brickwork of the cottages, head
down the track and into the woodland.

You are now on Shakespeare's Way, a
235km waymarked route running from the

◄ Stonor Park

Bard's birthplace in Stratford-upon-Avon to the Globe Theatre in London. It's doubtful whether the great man ever walked down this path, but it is fun to imagine that he did.

As you drop down the hillside and through a deer-proof gate into Stonor Park, keep an eye out for deer grazing in the parkland. You will get a fine view of the house, a family home to the Stonor family for 850 years. As staunch Catholics, the family suffered badly during the Reformation when they refused to recognise Henry VIII as head of the church.

The warm brick Georgian façade, seen clearly from across the valley, disguises the 12th-century origins of the house. Stonor has appeared on both large and small screens, most notably in the Bond movie *The Living Daylights*, in the TV version of *Hornblower* and, like most places around here, it has featured in *Midsomer Murders*.

In time, the path leads down to another deer-proof kissing gate to the left of the drive. Turn left to walk down through the village and back to the start point.

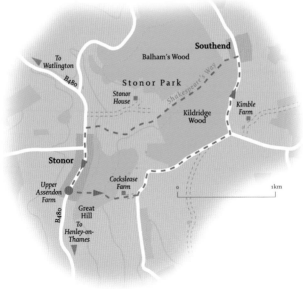

Swyncombe and Ewelme Park

Distance **5.6km** Time **2 hours**
Terrain **tracks, fields and woodland paths
higher up** Map **OS Explorer 171**
Access **no public transport to the start**

**It would be hard to find a more peaceful
corner of the Chilterns than the
Swyncombe parkland nestling in the
valley beside the 1000-year-old St
Botolph's Church. With mature trees on
the hilltop and rolling farmland on the
Ewelme Downs, this walking route
provides tranquillity and variety
regardless of the season.**

Swyncombe is a small hamlet 1.5km
west of Cookley Green. Park by the church
(RG9 6EA) and set off down the path
through the churchyard, leaving by the
gate on the far side. Turn left and walk up
to the drive to Swyncombe House.

A footpath sets off beside a wooden
fence and into the parkland. Head straight
across the pasture, making for a gate in
the treeline opposite. After just a few
paces, turn right on a path leading up
through the woods until you can turn
right again, where it merges with a track.

Cross a surfaced road and, soon
afterwards, take the path on the left as the
track drops downhill. Look out for a deep
sinkhole on your right just before you
leave the woods and re-enter the
parkland; there are lovely views over to
your right.

As you wander through the mature oak,
beech and chestnut trees, there are
delightful glimpses down to Swyncombe
House and farm. Keep close to the fence
on your left and it will lead to a corner of
the pasture. Go through the narrow strip
of woodland and turn left, now following
the Ridgeway Trail.

The path leads along the left edge of a
field and through a gap where it joins a

◄ Swyncombe

Swyncombe Downs

Down Farm

Ewelme Downs

Swyncombe

Swyncombe House

Haycroft Wood

Harcourt Hill

Ewelme Park

◄ To Wallingford

Harcourthill Shaw

A4130

To Henley-on-Thames

Chiltern Way

1km

track down to Ewelme Park. Turn left to walk between the buildings. Following signs for the Ridgeway, walk past the arched gatehouse to Ewelme House, through a gate and down the gentle slope. The path divides in the trees, but this route continues on the Ridgeway as directed by the signpost.

When you reach a field, look to the far side where a marker post in the distant bushes will guide you across. On entering the undergrowth on the other side, leave the Ridgeway and turn right, now on the Chiltern Way. This leads on through the bushes until it emerges onto a small patch of open ground with a lane over to your left.

Go right on the lane to walk up past the entrance to Harcourt Hill Shaw and out along the edge of a field, going gently uphill with a hedge on your right. When the ground levels out, take the opening on your right, beside a marker post, and walk over the brow of Harcourt Hill, keeping the hedge to your left.

The path leads down through a copse in the valley, across a track and on to join a surfaced driveway. Turn right and walk up through the trees until you are approaching stone gateposts. Bear left to a footpath which leads along the bottom of a field onto a path known as Ladies Walk. It leads into woods, then onto a track which runs along the valley all the way back to St Botolph's.

Christmas Common and Wormsley

Distance **11.5km** Time **3 hours 30**
Terrain **paths and tracks** Map **OS Explorer
171** Access **no public transport to the start**

**When one of the richest men in the
world chooses to make his home in the
Chilterns, you can be sure it is somewhere
special. Sir Paul Getty bought the
Wormsley Estate in 1986 and restored
the house and grounds regardless of
expense. Getty called it his 'Shangri-La'.
It is easy to see why.**

Cowleaze car park is about 5km west of
Stokenchurch (OX49 5HX). It has a height-
restricting barrier, although there is space
to park outside the entrance. From the
A40, take the road to Christmas Common
and you'll find the car park on the left-
hand side after 3km.

From the vehicle entrance, head into the
woods between wooden stumps. Stick to
the main path across a clearing, using
white arrows painted on trees to guide

you through the trees to a gate. Keep left
of the nearest electricity pole as you cross
two fields. Turn left onto a lane.

After 50m, a wooden gate in a hedge on
the right leads past the front of Lower
Vicar's Farm, and up the other side of the
valley. With the farm down to your left,
enter woodland and go uphill to a
crossroads. Turn right onto a wide path
and walk downhill for the next 1km to the
well-kept driveway to Wormsley House.

Turn right where, after 500m, the drive
goes right and a track heads off to the left.
Between the two is the famous cricket
ground built by Getty after he was
introduced to the game by Mick Jagger.
It is close, but remains out of sight.

Go left along the track onto a path,
keeping a fence at your left-hand side.
Where the path forks, you might want to
walk uphill between fences for a short
distance to look back over the cricket
ground and parkland. To continue the

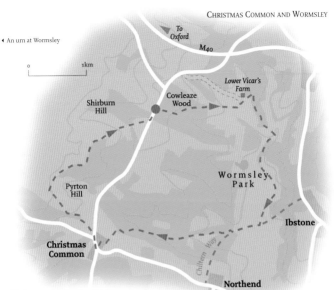

◀ An urn at Wormsley

walk, however, take the right-hand path to carry on with a meadow sloping up to your left.

After about 500m, turn right through a gate to cross a field to a lane. Cross over and walk to the corner of the next field before turning right onto the next lane. After a few paces, take the footpath on the left to walk beside Wormsley's walled garden. Fork right to cross a clearing with an impressive ornamental urn, and head into the trees.

The path winds gently uphill for the next 1.7km with white arrows on trees to help you. At the top follow the path, keeping close to a field on your left, to join a track leading left past a house. At the bottom of the garden, turn right to a road. Go right for 200m where, before the speed limit signs, a footpath heads left into the hedge.

Walk along the side of two fields to a gate in the corner, where you turn left, downhill. The path joins a tarmac lane and passes the gates of a sawmill. Look for a little gate in the hedge on your right which leads across grasslands, first among bushes and then into trees until you are walking along the edge of woods, with fields to your left.

The path finally veers to the right, away from the field edge, to Shirburn Hill. You will see the route climbing the slope to a gate at the top right corner. Cross a field to a road and turn left. Once past a watertower on the right, step into the woods to walk beside the road to the start.

Watlington to Lewknor

Distance 9.5km **Time** 3 hours
Terrain paths, tracks and country roads
Map OS Explorer 171 **Access** buses from
Oxford and Reading to Watlington

Watlington is a characterful market town,
full of history and interest. On a hill
overlooking it is a strange triangle cut into
the slopes. In the 18th century, the local
squire felt that the parish church would
look better from his house if it had a spire,
so he created the illusion of one by
commissioning the 82m hillside feature
known as the Watlington White Mark.

Start from the public car park on Hill
Road (OX49 5BD). Turn right to walk
beside the road, past the Carriers Arms on
your left and a row of houses on your
right. Soon the White Mark appears on the
hillside ahead.

Leave the road just before it bends out
of sight to go left onto the Ridgeway Trail,
although it shares this section with the
Icknield Way and the Swan's Way. For the
next 3.5km, simply follow the path with
the Chiltern escarpment over to your right
on a route which has been used for
thousands of years.

In time, the path leaves the trees and
continues between hedges, with Shirburn
Hill on the right, and the M40 emerges
from the hillside ahead. The deep cutting
made to accommodate the motorway was
hugely controversial when it was
constructed in the 1970s, not only slicing
through an Area of Outstanding Natural
Beauty, but also running through the
middle of the Aston Rowant National
Nature Reserve.

As you walk towards the motorway, a
signpost in the hedge on the left directs
you onto a footpath, marked L13, towards
the distinctive profile of a watertank on a
knoll. Leave the tank to your left to walk

◀ Pyrton lychgate

to a road. Turn left, heading downhill to the B4009.

Cross with care and go left to a lay-by, where a concrete path takes you down the bank to a quiet lane leading into Lewknor. Go straight over the crossroads, passing Ye Olde Leathern Bottel pub, into Weston Road. Follow the road for 1.5km out of the village to Manor Farm, with sheds on the left and a brick and flint farmhouse on the right. Take the minor road on the left, called Rectory Lane, bearing right at the gates of a house to walk with gardens to your left.

Continue along the edge of a field, turning left over a footbridge and then right to an opening in the hedge ahead. Go left to the field corner, then turn right down to the access track to Model Farm, with its industrial appearance and tall chimney. Face the farm buildings and look to your immediate right where a path leads down the side of the field behind a stout fence to a lane.

Cross to the corner of a field and aim for the opposite corner, doing the same over the next field. Turn right onto a track to walk along the edge of a field, crossing another track and continuing until you come to Pyrton. Turn left at the road junction to walk up through the village.

Shortly before the speed limit signs, turn right to walk along a road for 500m to a footpath sign pointing left along a field edge. Take this before bearing right to pass between allotments and a school. Go right on the road past the Chequers pub to follow Chapel Street up to the High Street. A left turn will take you to Watlington's town hall with the car park just beyond.

The south of Buckinghamshire is perhaps most at risk from the pressures of being so close to the city of London. Yet it has survived remarkably unscathed.

Centres of population like High Wycombe, Marlow and Amersham have provided a focus for development and groups such as the Chiltern Society have done much to preserve the character of the surrounding villages and countryside. Nevertheless, the government caused a furore back in the 1970s when it cut through the hills to construct the M40 motorway. The Stokenchurch Gap, over 1km long and almost 50m deep, carved through both public opinion and a National Nature Reserve to create a fast road between London and Oxford.

Today the Stokenchurch Gap is a Site of Special Scientific Interest and it is surprisingly easy for the walker to ignore, with the traffic noise quickly absorbed by the ever-present woodland.

Travelling south towards the border with Berkshire, the ancient woodland of the Burnham Beeches provides yet another magical retreat from the urban areas that surround it.

Marlow to Chorleywood

Burnham Beeches

Distance **5.5km** Time **2 hours**
Terrain **woodland paths and fields**
Map **OS Explorer 172** Access **buses from Slough and High Wycombe stop at Farnham Common, 500m from the start**

It's odd to find yourself in a City of London car park so far from the capital, but if it wasn't for London the ancient woodland of Burnham Beeches would no longer exist. Saved from developers in 1880, London has managed the woods ever since. It's a magical place – used as a location for one of the *Harry Potter* films – with a network of paths to explore, and it is surprisingly easy to lose the crowds.

Parking is free from Monday to Friday at the car park opposite Beeches Road, just off the A355 in Farnham Common (SL2 3LB). Walk up past the café to a

crossroads, known as Victory Cross, where you turn left onto Sir Henry Peek's Drive. At a cattle grid, go left to walk for 200m beside a fence. A gate opens to the right, onto a boardwalk over wetlands known as the Mire.

When the boardwalk ends at a junction of paths, go straight over, turning right at a T-junction. Cross Sir Henry Peek's Drive and walk to a wide gravel path leading through the woods to Middle Pond. With the water to your right, head past the end of the pond and go left at the fork.

Look out for the 800-year-old Druid's Oak behind a fence to your right as you aim for a wooden shelter by a road called Lord Mayor's Drive. This area is known as Sevenways Plain and is the site of a prehistoric hillfort. More recently, in the Second World War, it was used to conceal

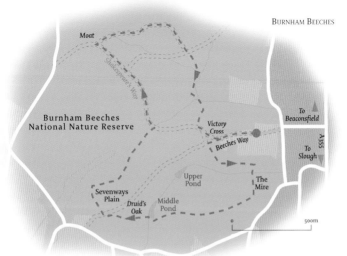

a stockpile of vehicles from enemy spotter planes before the D-Day landings.

Go past the front of the shelter, keeping the wooden fence to your right, and follow the path up through the trees. Where it veers away from the fence, you will arrive at a crossing of paths. The route here goes downhill to the left, but you might enjoy a detour through the gate a few paces to your right.

This opens into grassland with fine examples of the huge, gnarly old beech and oak pollards for which the Burnham Beeches are famous, including one of the best known trees in the country, the Cage Pollard. Since it appeared in the 1991 film *Robin Hood: Prince of Thieves* with Kevin Costner, steel beams have been added to help support the branches.

Returning to the crossroads, head downhill as described above. This takes you down Mendelssohn's Slope, where it

is said the composer had the inspiration for Puck and Oberon's incidental music to William Shakespeare's play *A Midsummer Night's Dream*.

At the bottom of the valley, go left to a road, called Halse Drive. You can bear right on the road for a shortcut home, but this route goes left. Walk up the hill, past Duke's Drive, to a crossroads by another wooden shelter. A few metres to your right, along McAullife Drive, is Hartley Court Moat, dating from between the 12th and 14th centuries.

Follow the road downhill to a junction by a Corporation of London information board. Ignore the roads to either side and head on downhill on a rough track bending slowly to the right. At a junction of several paths, go left down to a footbridge and follow the path back up the other side to Victory Cross. The café is over to your left.

◀ Pollard in Burnham Beeches

Marlow Common

Distance 7.5km Time 2 hours 30
Terrain woodland paths
Map OS Explorer 172 Access no public
transport to the start

A glorious woodland walk, full of variety
and interest, with an opportunity to see
England's best-preserved network of
First World War training trenches.

From Marlow, take the A4155 towards
Henley, turning right for Marlow
Common just as you leave the town. After
1.5km, go right at the fork to park under
the trees (SL7 2DS). Three lanes come
together at this point to form a triangle.
Walk down to the lowest corner of the
triangle, and take a wide path which
begins between wooden posts, heading
away from the road. This leads through
woods to a marker post.

Ignore the pointers and turn right past

an area of regenerating woodland, aiming
for the edge of the woods. Just before a
post, which marks the entrance to a
housing estate, go right and follow the
path to a fork. Go left and left again soon
after to join another path, with the
housing estate to your left. Where the
path leads out of the woods into the
housing estate, bear right to follow the
edge of the woods to a lane.

Go right to walk with an impressive flint
wall of a garden centre to your left. Where
the wall ends, look for a footpath on the
right, just past a brick garage. This heads
down to the valley bottom where you turn
right and follow the path up the edge of
the woodland. Ignore paths to the left or
right to reach a road after 1.25km. Here,
turn left and go round the corner, joining a
path on the right which continues up the
valley to a junction of paths after 500m.

‹ WWI training trenches in Marlow Common

Turn left to walk beside the hedge, then with hedges on both sides (and overhead) until you turn left between fences along the edge of a field. Turn right at a road and then left into Homefield Wood just around the corner.

At the Red Kite information board, a gate onto a permissive footpath to your right leads uphill through conifers into mixed woodland. Cross a track, then fork right before crossing a valley. When you emerge into a field, go right along the edge to a gap in the hedge by a house. Cross the road onto a footpath bearing right across a field.

Make for the window of the house peeking through the trees to stay on the right of way. Turn right along the road and, after 80m, take a narrow footpath going left between high garden fences to a field. Walk downhill, crossing an access track, then head up the field on the other side, bearing right to join a footpath in the top corner.

This leads to a bridleway beside an information board for Marlow Common. Turn right along the bridleway to a road junction, then go left. After 100m a track cuts back on your right, leading past

Monks Corner and a distinctive white house with terracotta friezes, best known as the former home of *Three Men in a Boat* author Jerome K Jerome. Cross the road and turn left to return to the start. Don't miss the trench network which is set back from the road. There are around 1400m of trenches here, built by the Grenadier Guards in the First World War to train troops before they were sent to the front.

Cadmore End, Fingest and Turville

Distance 5km **Time** 2 hours
Terrain footpath and tracks with climbs
and descents **Map** OS Explorer 171
Access buses from High Wycombe and
Stokenchurch to Cadmore End

Cadmore End is just a stone's throw
from the M40, but you wouldn't know it.
This walk takes you to two unspoilt
communities nestling in the hills.
It's not a long walk, but it includes a
couple of very steep hills, so there are
two descents and two lung-busting
climbs. You won't regret it because the
views are glorious and the villages
embody the England of Agatha Christie's
Miss Marple (without the murders).

Park by the side of the track opposite the
school (HP14 3PE). Walk up the track, soon
passing St Mary-Le-Moor Church. The
footpath begins over to the right by the

farm gate at the end of a garden hedge.
Follow this as it leads past a field and then
sets off downhill between hedges, before
rising again into Hanger Wood.

Go right at a fork on the edge of the
wood to head slightly uphill. Ignore a
path to the right and continue to follow
the main path, going straight on at the
next junction. At the next fork, go right
for the first steep descent, with views
opening out across the valley. The path
emerges in Fingest beside a typically
picturesque Chilterns cottage.

Head left along the road, turning right
in front of the Chequers pub. The 12th-
century St Bartholomew's Church on your
right is famous for its 'saddle-back' tower,
with double gables. There is only one
other in England like it. After the
churchyard gate, take the footpath which
cuts up to the right, with a flint wall on

◄ Hanger Wood, Cadmore End

your left. Bear left in the woods, but not before sneaking a look back towards the church. There is a lovely view over the gate which shows off the tower set against the hills in the background.

After crossing a road, walk along the hillside into a field with the village of Turville over to the left. As you make your way over the field to a gate in the corner, the Cobstone windmill is on the skyline to your right. It has featured on TV and films a number of times, most famously as the home of Caractacus Potts in the 1968 film, *Chitty Chitty Bang Bang*. Now in private hands, it is easier to see it from the valley floor than the top of the hill.

At the corner of the field, pass through the gate with Turville, a cluster of period cottages grouped around a green and flanked by a pub and church, over to the left. Often used as a set location, perhaps most famously in the BBC series *The Vicar of Dibley*, it is well worth a pit stop but if you just wish to continue, head right to tackle a relentlessly steep hill.

Near the top, the path dog-legs slightly left as you keep to the fence by the windmill. Turn right at the road for a few paces to rejoin the footpath as

it dives into the woods to your left. Follow it downhill, keeping close to the wooden fence, to meet a road.

Turn right and, after about 80m, a footpath bears left – the second steep climb of the walk – up a field and into woods. At the top, go left at a marker post to emerge onto the track you walked earlier by the edge of Hanger Wood. Turn left and retrace your steps to the start.

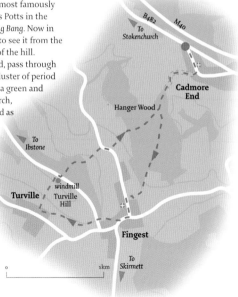

Tylers Green, Penn and the Royal Standard

Distance **7.2km** Time **2 hours 30**
Terrain **paths, tracks, brief sections of public road and fields** Map **OS Explorer 172**
Access **buses from High Wycombe stop opposite the Red Lion in Tylers Green**

In the Middle Ages, Penn was the centre of England's tile-making industry. Local people had the right to dig free clay from the green and so part of the parish became known as Tylers Green. With a pub, a pond, a couple of shops and a garage selling supercars, it makes a good starting point for this walk.

Park by the pond at Tylers Green and head down the lane to the left of the Red Lion (HP10 8LF). At Puttenham Place Farm, take the path on the right to walk round buildings into a field.

Go left for a few metres to join a path leading right beside a hedge up to Brook Wood. Keep right of the trees for 50m to a path dropping downhill to your right into Penn Bottom, then up the other side through Vicarage Woods. It emerges beside the Crown Inn.

Go right, past the pub, then cross the road into a lane called Pauls Hill. After 300m, take the footpath on the left of the entrance to Bede House which leads between fields to a surfaced lane. Turn right and follow it until it bends left to a house. Ahead is a gate which leads onto a path to the left of farm buildings. It will take you along the edge of the woods to a marker post, where you turn right.

Cross the grass until you are walking with a hedge at your right hand to reach a gate. This opens onto a narrow path to a road at Forty Green. On the right is the Royal Standard of England, a pub which can trace its history back some 900 years.

◄ The Royal Standard of England

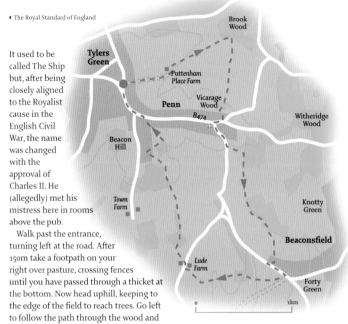

It used to be called The Ship but, after being closely aligned to the Royalist cause in the English Civil War, the name was changed with the approval of Charles II. He (allegedly) met his mistress here in rooms above the pub.

Walk past the entrance, turning left at the road. After 150m take a footpath on your right over pasture, crossing fences until you have passed through a thicket at the bottom. Now head uphill, keeping to the edge of the field to reach trees. Go left to follow the path through the wood and across two fields, turning right at the track up to Lude Farm.

Turn right on the road and then left onto a footpath after the farm buildings. Cross a field to the right-hand corner to turn right into woods. Take the left path at the fork to walk up through the conifers. After passing through a wooden gate, keep to the right side of the field with young trees to your left. Go through the next patch of woodland, passing a hollow on your left, then skirt round the left side of a field.

Follow the path up the fenceline and into a dark tunnel of leylandii to the drive of a house called Whitecroft. Go left for 30m, looking for a footpath which sets off to the right. Go down the slope and up again to turn left after a wooden gate. The path now goes uphill between gardens, ever-narrowing until you reach Church Road.

Cross over and head left to return to the green at Tylers Green. You will pass Slade's Garage on the way – handy if you want to pick up a Ferrari or Aston Martin as a souvenir of your day out.

West Wycombe and Bradenham

Distance **7km** Time **2 hours 30**
Terrain **tracks and woodland paths**
Map **OS Explorer 172** Access **buses from
High Wycombe and Stokenchurch to
West Wycombe**

These villages are both owned by the
National Trust, but are very different in
character. West Wycombe oozes 18th-
century charm, in spite of straddling the
busy A40, while Bradenham is a simple
cluster of buildings around a village
green. With spectacular attractions along
the way, this is an exciting expedition.

Park at the former garden centre on the
Chorley Road out of West Wycombe (HP14
3AP). Take the path opposite the entrance,
bearing right over the grass to reach
Church Lane, with the Hellfire Caves just
along the road to the left.

They were created by the 18th-century
libertine Sir Francis Dashwood and

became a base for his infamous Hellfire
Club. Step onto the grass beyond the caves
and walk up the hill to the Dashwood
Mausoleum and St Lawrence's Church.
Both were created by Dashwood, with the
golden ball on the church capable of
seating several people and allegedly used
for occasional club meetings!

Beyond the church is a car park, at the
far end of which a track heads along the
left side of the ridge. After about 1km, go
right at a fork and continue along the
broad track until you reach Nobles Farm.
Opposite the entrance, at the corner of a
wooden fence, a path goes right, leading
downhill and along the edge of a
meadow. Go through bushes in the corner
and head right to walk along the top edge
of a field to a gate into a small paddock.
Now bear left to the opposite corner
where the path leads under the railway
before bearing left to a gate onto the road.

◄ Dashwood Mausoleum

Cross the busy carriageway with care and go right to the junction. Now turn left and walk up Bradenham Wood Lane until you can cross the green below the cricket pitch. In the top corner, to the right of Bradenham Manor garden, a track heads uphill. Walk up to the corner of the garden wall where a narrow path sets off to your right, leading up the bank into the trees.

There is a white square painted on a tree as you continue to walk across and up the hillside. When you join a rough track running up the hill, turn left for a few steps, then turn right to rejoin the path. You will walk between dense holly bushes as the path winds through the woodland to join another track. Turn right to walk on level ground until you can take a path on the right as the track bends left.

Soon you go downhill, through yew trees, then an avenue of beeches and finally between fences to a gate above the railway track. Go left on the path and, after a few hundred metres, turn right at a junction where you will be able to pass under the railway to cross a field to the road. A gate on the other side opens into a paddock and allows you to follow the path towards the opposite corner.

A small gate, a few metres down the left-hand side and rather hidden in the hedge, lets you through to the pavement. Turn right to walk up through West Wycombe village. The entrance to West Wycombe Park – created by Sir Francis, of course – is on the left at the top of the village, and your start point is just a short walk further on.

Hughenden

Distance **7km** Time **2 hours 30**
Terrain **tracks, paths and a little bit of
pavement** Map **OS Explorer 172**
Access **buses from High Wycombe
and Stokenchurch**

**Hughenden is inexorably linked with
Benjamin Disraeli, Queen Victoria's
favourite prime minister. He lived in the
house and is buried in the churchyard. As
relief from the burdens of his high office,
Disraeli loved to walk the parkland that
surrounded his home. It's easy to see why.**

If you are a member of the National
Trust, there is free parking at Hughenden.
Otherwise, you can leave your car in
Commonside, Downley, to the east of the
Bricklayers Arms (HP13 5XJ).

With the grass and trees to your left,
walk along Commonside, turning right

into Littleworth Road. Follow the
pavement for 200m to a footpath on the
left, immediately after Number 78. It leads
across a private drive before dropping into
Little Tinker's Wood.

Go left when you enter the woods, then
right at the fork and follow the path up
the hill to a metal gate opening into a
field with the D'Israeli monument ahead.
This was erected by Disraeli's wife, Mary-
Anne, to her father-in-law, Isaac D'Israeli.
It commands fine views to the house.

When ready, return through the gate
and turn right to follow the path on the
edge of the woods down to a gate at the
bottom of the hill. Go into the field to
walk with the fence at your right hand
over to Coates Lane. Turn left, then right
after 30m onto a track leading uphill.

Hughenden Valley

At Middle Lodge, step to the left to enter the parkland via metal gates, then head right to walk down the hill to the stream at the bottom. Turn left to follow the stream (which sometimes dries up) to a gate in a metal fence. Bear left across the slope, keeping above the church and houses until you reach the drive. This is the closest the route passes to Hughenden Manor – the drive leads up to the house and gardens which are now in the care of the National Trust and open to visitors (admission fee). To continue the walk, turn right when you reach the drive, heading uphill for a short distance until you can join a footpath on the right, signposted for Naphill, beside a cottage. This leads up to a marker post with a red arrow. Turn right and, as directed by the arrows, go through Woodcock Wood to a metal gate.

The path goes slightly left from here, across the corner of a meadow. After another gate, walk with a hedge initially to your right, before you cross a track (the Coffin Path) and continue with the hedge now on your left. The path leads round to the right, beside Flagmore Wood; ignore a stile on your left to reach a gate into the trees. Now follow the path to another red arrow after about 400m to head downhill.

At the bottom, go left on a wide bridleway that leads towards a field gate. Just before the gate, turn right on a path up through trees into a deep ditch. Keep the ditch to your right as you drop down the slope, cross a track and continue up the other side. The path leads through the woods to emerge between fences onto the road, opposite a sign for Coates Lane. Your car, or bus stop, is a short walk along Commonside to the right.

◀ Hughenden

Old Amersham and the Martyrs

Distance **9km** Time **2 hours 30**
Terrain **paths and farm tracks**
Map **OS Explorer 172** Access **buses from
Chesham and High Wycombe to Old
Amersham's High Street; Amersham's
Railway Station is 1.5km from the start**

Amersham, or 'Old Amersham' as it has
come to be called these days, should not
be confused with its younger, brasher –
and frankly less attractive – neighbour up
the hill. The old town is a delight, with
its broad main street flanked by coaching
inns, almshouses, the parish church and
a 17th-century market hall. Amersham-
on-the-Hill, on the other hand, has a
history no older than the railway, but it
does make it easy to join this walk from
the station.

There is a pay and display car park just
off The Broadway, close to Tesco (HP7
0HL). Walk back to the street and turn left
to cross the supermarket access road
at a roundabout, then continue

along the pavement for about 40m. On
the other side of the road is Bury Cottage,
and the path begins on the gravel drive
immediately to its right.

Walk to a gate into a field and on to an
underpass beneath the A413. After a
further 150m go through a gate in the
hedge which opens into a field. The path
heads uphill to the left and across the
corner of a wood. Continue across the
next fields with Quarrenden Farm to your
right and Day's Wood ahead. Keep to the
right of Day's Wood to reach a waymarker
at the far corner.

The path crosses the next field, bearing
right to a gate in a hedge. As you head
over the brow, the buildings of Upper
Bottom House Farm gradually appear.
Go through the farmyard and turn left
down the lane to Lower Bottom House

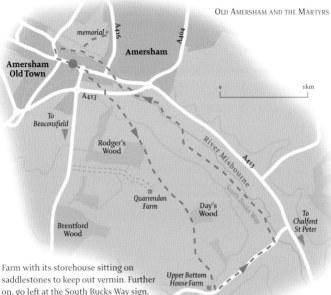

Farm with its storehouse sitting on saddlestones to keep out vermin. Further on, go left at the South Bucks Way sign.

With the Misbourne River to your right, the path skirts around fields, then passes woods and a hedge on your right before you aim straight ahead across a field, still on the South Bucks Way. On meeting a flinty track, follow it right to cross the river before immediately turning left to walk with the river by your left hand.

This leads to woodland and through an underpass before you arrive at a road close to Ambers of Amersham. Cross this to pass the front of the Chequers pub and through the courtyard to the right of Ambers. A narrow lane takes you to a road.

Cross over and follow the cyclepath until you see a sign for the Martyrs Memorial, pointing right. The path leads up the slope to reach the memorial.

Erected in 1931, it commemorates seven local 'dissenters' found guilty of heresy for reading the Bible in English translation and burned at the stake in the early 1500s. It was a time of great cruelty and persecution; the daughter of one of the martyrs was forced to light her father's pyre herself.

To reach Amersham Station from here, take the path round to Station Road and turn left. Otherwise, return to the cyclepath, turning right to pass a cemetery on your right. Cross the brick bridge and keep to the right of the church. Turn left on Church Street to the Market Hall. Go left along The Broadway to the start.

◀ Grain store on Lower Bottom Farm

Sarratt to Chenies

Distance 7.5km **Time** 3 hours 30
Terrain paths, fields and quiet lanes
Map OS Explorer 172 **Access** buses from
Watford and Hemel Hempstead to Sarratt

Sarratt Green and Chenies are two very
different villages. The former dates from
medieval times when it was a popular
drovers' route, with grazing and ponds to
keep the livestock happy and five taverns
to refresh the drovers. Now it has fewer
pubs but otherwise has changed
remarkably little since those days.
Chenies, which can trace its history back
to Saxon times, used to be entirely
owned by the Duke of Bedford until the
family sold it in the 1950s. Combining the
two with the picturesque River Chess
makes this walk hard to beat.

Park on the roadside in Sarratt Green
and make your way to the Cricketers pub
(WD3 6AS). You can't miss its magnificent
sign standing proudly at the side of the
road. Walk up past the pond where a
footpath sign directs you left into a lane
between houses.

Pass the village school on your left and
go through a gate to walk along the side
of some fields, following a path that leads
into Sandfield Wood. Cross a lane and
bear left over a field, making for the right-
hand end of a hedge on the far side. Take
the gate on your right before turning left
to walk downhill to the river, following
signs to Chenies.

A footbridge helps you over the River
Chess to reach another footbridge and a
gate into the woods. As soon as you step
into the trees, bear right onto a path
which cuts directly across a field to the far
hedge. Turn left at the hedge, then right

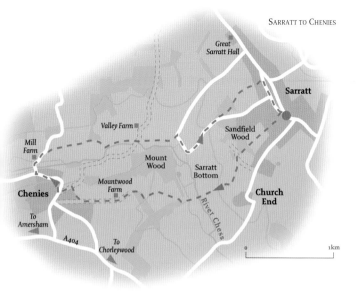

at the corner to follow field edges up past the buildings at Mountwood Farm, and down the drive. Some 100m after the gates, take a path on the right which leads down behind some stables to Holloway Lane. Turn left and walk along it to the public road.

The village of Chenies is a short detour to the left, but the path resumes across the road, beside the sign warning of a bend in the road. It takes you down the hill, ending at a flight of steps where it rejoins the road. Cross carefully, then go left to walk along the roadside until you can turn right to a bridge over the river. Stay on the road until it starts to go uphill. Take the path on your right here, heading between fences with the river over to the right. This leads through

Frogmore Wood and on along the edge of fields to Tyler and Sons' Watercress Beds, the last commercial watercress beds on the river.

The path becomes a concrete track at this point and leads to a road junction where you turn right towards Sarratt Bottom, keeping parallel to the river. After 200m, turn left to walk up Dawes Lane, passing Cakebread Cottage and ignoring the gate just above it. As you climb the hill, the lane enters woodland where a path leads uphill through the trees.

Cross a path when you come to it and go into the field at the top of the wood. Keep to the right-hand side of a hedge to reach the top corner where the path leads past the houses and out onto the green. Turn right for the Cricketers.

◄ The Cricketers by Sarratt Green

Chorleywood

Distance **6.7km** Time **2 hours 30**
Terrain **tracks and footpaths**
Map **OS Explorer 172** Access **buses from
the town centre stop at the Stag pub**

**Contrasts could not be clearer on this trip
to the south of Chorleywood. Setting out
from a pub on the edge of town into the
rolling countryside, it's hard not to pity
the poor souls on the nearby M25. Quiet
and varied, this walk provides an ideal
opportunity to visit the Chiltern Open
Air Museum.**

The Stag pub is easy to find from the
M25; go west at Junction 17 and it's 1.5km
along Long Lane on the left. Park in Stag
Lane opposite the pub (WD3 5BT).

Facing the pub's front door, take the
track to the right, passing allotments. Go
left at a fork, cross a stile and then turn
left on a footpath between a hedge and a

fence. It runs under a canopy of
overhanging oak boughs for almost 1km.
The hum of the M25 grows louder as you
near the motorway, but don't worry, it'll
soon be behind you and muffled by trees.

Cross a stile, with Bottom Wood to your
right and the motorway just visible
beyond. Although the right of way
demands you continue straight ahead
until you are around 100m from the
motorway before cutting back, if the field
is in pasture it is possible to turn right
after the stile and walk across to the
woods, before turning left to follow the
field edge round two corners to the
entrance into the woods. Take the path
leading up through the trees.

Ignoring any paths that cross your trail,
keep heading in roughly the same
direction and you will emerge at the
southwestern corner of the wood at a

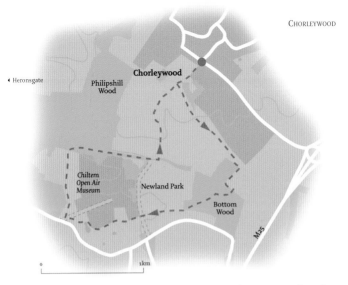

◄ Heronsgate

Chorleywood

Philipshill
Wood

Chiltern
Open Air
Museum

Newland Park

Bottom
Wood

M25

0   1km

gate. Turn right to skirt along the edge of the field and cross the farm road to a gate in the corner. Please note: at this point the path now crosses parkland belonging to a former college campus which is being redeveloped for residential housing. The route is liable to change as the development progresses, in which case you should follow official footpath signs to reach the main drive to Newland Park.

Until then, go across a footpath and onto playing fields, initially with an artificial surface to your right. Pass through a gate in the far hedge, which leads onto parkland, with buildings on your right. Turn right when you are able and then bear left to a gate. Cross the drive to Newland Manor and look slightly left where a gate opens onto a footpath across a field. Over to your right is the

Chiltern Open Air Museum – well worth a visit if you have time.

The path leads into woods in the left corner of the field. Bear right through the trees to a track. Turn right (both the track and the footpath beside it lead to the same spot) to join Old Shire Lane. Go right and follow the lane out of the woods. Ignore the path on the right, but continue ahead for 100m to Bullsland Lane. Turn left up the slope with a degraded concrete surface.

Where the lane bends left, take the gate onto the pasture to the right and follow the path across a field, through another gate and on uphill, bearing slightly right to reach a gate in the far fence. After going through this and across the stile, you will recognise the lane leading back past the allotments to the Stag.

49

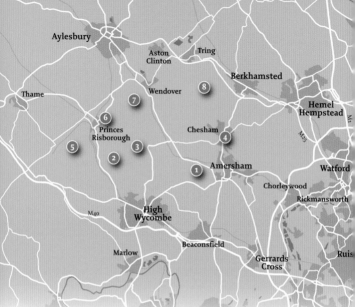

Nowhere in the Chilterns are the views more spectacular than along the northwestern escarpment, and few are better than those which look out over the Vale of Aylesbury.

From Bledlow to Wendover the steep hillside makes a clear distinction between the agricultural plains of the Vale and the woods and downlands of the Chiltern Hills. Haddington Hill near Wendover claims to be the highest point in the Chilterns at 267m, although the other lesser summits, such as Coombe and Whiteleaf Hills, and along the Bledlow Ridge, offer better vantage points.

Tucked in the valley below one of the most famous viewpoints is Chequers, the prime minister's country retreat, with public footpaths passing remarkably close to the house and gardens. For the railway enthusiast, steam locomotives puff their way from Chinnor to Princes Risborough, while the London Underground's Metropolitan Line extends as far as Chesham, making the capital a mere hour's tube ride away.

Between the two are charming villages like Great Missenden, where Roald Dahl lived for much of his life, and historic buildings like Hampden House, once home to Oliver Cromwell's cousin, a leading figure in the build-up to the Civil War. Woods, windmills and wonderful walking trails are just waiting to be explored.

Ellesborough ▶

Around Princes Risborough and Chesham

Little Missenden

Distance **6.5km** Time **2 hours**
Terrain **footpaths and pasture**
Map **OS Explorer 172** Access **buses from
Amersham to Little Missenden**

Little Missenden is a gem of a village,
boasting a 13th-century church, a
Jacobean manor house, a village hall, a
school and two pubs. It sits on the River
Misbourne which had all but disappeared
by 1990, sucked dry by pumping stations
which diverted its clear, clean
groundwater into the public water
supply. The authorities took steps to
reverse the decline and, although the
river can still dwindle to a trickle in dry
weather, its resurrection is a great
success story.

Park on the roadside in Little Missenden
and head for the village hall which is at
the east end of the village opposite the
Crown Inn (HP7 0RD). To the left of the
hall is a track called Toby's Lane which is
signposted as the Chiltern Heritage Trail.
It sets off past a characterful cottage on
the left-hand side, becoming a path as it
enters the woods.

Toby's Lane is an ancient path which
leads gently up the hillside. When the
ground begins to level off, take the
wooden gate on the left and bear right to
a gap in the hedgerow, cutting off the
corner of the field. Take the same line
across the next field, turning right when
you reach the track to Mop End Farm. At
the start of an avenue of trees, cross into

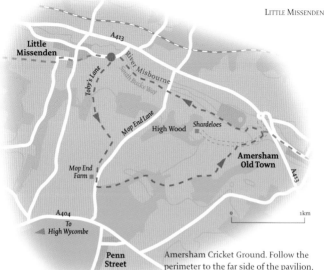

the field on your left and walk up the right-hand side to a stile in the top corner.

Go right on the road for 80m, then take the footpath which is signposted to the left through the beechwoods. Walk down round a pylon (there is a substantial electricity substation in the trees to your right) and follow the path as it meanders down the hillside and into a field at the bottom. The path ahead runs along the valley bottom, joining a track where you walk with woods by your right hand until the track bends down to the right.

Now go straight ahead to walk along a sparse line of trees with the odd solid horse jump to your right to reach a gate onto the private drive to Shardeloes House. Turn right and follow the drive downhill until you can turn left into Amersham Cricket Ground. Follow the perimeter to the far side of the pavilion, where a path dives into the trees. Soon you will be walking with Shardeloes Lake to your right and the house dominating the hill to your left.

The impressive mansion, built by the wonderfully named Stiff Leadbetter, is now divided into separate residences but was originally commissioned as a private home for the local MP William Drake.

From here you walk along the valley, enjoying parkland laid out by Humphry Repton in 1793. Repton, regarded as the last of the great 18th-century landscape architects, also dammed the Misbourne to form the lake to your right. As you progress along the valley floor, the path joins a farm track before meeting the public road at the eastern end of Little Missenden. Take a left turn and, after 100m, the Crown Inn will be on your right.

Lacey Green

Distance **7.5km** Time **2 hours 30**
Terrain **quiet roads, fields and tracks**
Maps **OS Explorer 172 and 181**
Access **buses from Aylesbury and High
Wycombe stop at the Whip in Lacey Green,
where you can join the walk midway**

**Standing by the iconic windmill at Lacey
Green, it's hard to believe it was a
complete ruin half a century ago.
Volunteers saved and restored it to
working condition. Open on Sundays and
Bank Holiday Mondays during the
summer months, it's easy to admire at
any time of the year and is a highlight of
this wonderful exploration of the
Chiltern countryside.**

There is a car park in Small Dean Lane,
accessed by driving south from Lacey
Green, turning right at the first crossroads
and going to the bottom of the hill. The
car park is on the left (HP27 0PR).

Step back onto the lane and, being wary
of traffic, go left. Take a footpath which

sets off to the right, 100m past Small Dean
Farm. Climb uphill to the end of a hedge,
then walk with the hedge at your right
hand. Follow the path around the field
edges, with views over Saunderton to the
Bledlow Ridge, until the hedge ends and
you find yourself crossing the hillside,
alongside a fence. The path ends at an
unusual metal stile, with adverts
embossed in the steps.

Turn right and walk up the road before
turning right into Loosley Hill. At the top
is the Whip Inn with England's oldest
smock windmill just behind – 350 years
old and still going strong, thanks to
volunteers from the Chiltern Society. Turn
right when facing the Whip and walk
300m down the Main Road before turning
left into Goodacres Lane.

Go straight ahead when the lane
becomes a track and follow it round to the
right. Walk along the edge of the field
until you pass a house on your left.
Immediately after, a track turns left to

◄ Small Dean Farm

bend downhill, but if you take a few more paces you can head left down Grim's Ditch. This Iron Age construction was made by digging a trench and using the spoil to build a bank beside it, probably as a way of marking out territory. You can find Grim's Ditches or Dykes all across southern England.

Where the ditch crosses a track, go right and follow the track, now called Kiln Lane, heading downhill for over 1km, past a row of houses on the left at Highwood Bottom. Ignore the first footpath on your right but take the second, just before the first house on the right. A sign points the way, although it is also hard to spot.

Climb the hill, bearing left to cross a

stile. Then hug the hedge as you follow it round to a track. Go left to join a road after 300m. Turn right and walk round the corner where a stile lets you cross a field on the right. Head to the far left corner, then bear left to walk past playing fields to a main road.

Cross over and take the footpath to your left. This leads through a field, beside another section of Grim's Dyke, and onto Small Dean Lane. Turn right. As the lane starts dropping more steeply downhill, a gate on your left opens into Small Dean Bank. Follow the path through the trees for 200m until a gate on your right lets you walk down the hillside back to the car park at the start.

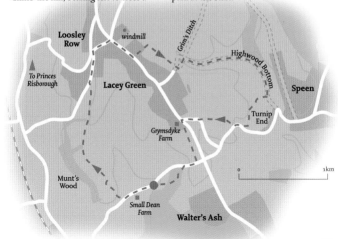

Hampden

Distance 8.5km **Time** 3 hours
Terrain paths and some lanes
Map OS Explorer 181 **Access** buses from
High Wycombe to Hampden on Tuesday,
Wednesday and schooldays

**The Elizabethan house at the centre of the
Hampden Estate has a history stretching
back to the 14th century. It has hosted
royalty, helped start a revolution and been
a 'house of horror' on many occasions.
Steeped in history and scenic countryside,
this walk is not to be missed.**

The Hampden Arms makes an ideal start
point and the landlord is happy for walkers
to use the car park to work up a thirst
(HP16 9RQ). Alternatively, park at the
roadside at the far end of Memorial Road.

From the pub, head round to the left
along Memorial Road, crossing a lopsided
crossroads to walk to a road junction. By
the triangle of grass in the middle of the

junction, take the footpath leading into
bushes. It emerges to follow the edge of a
field beside trees, before heading across
arable land to a clump of bushes.

Turn right to walk beside the hedge,
into trees and down to a lane. Cross to a
path under the trees on the other side.
When you can, step left to walk up the
side of the fields until you reach a
wooden fence with a marker post and
stile. Cross the stile and continue towards
Honor End Farm, bearing right before the
buildings to a gate onto a road. Turn left
and walk 100m to the memorial on the
right. It commemorates John Hampden,
one of five parliamentarians whose
attempted arrest by King Charles I for
high treason led to the outbreak of the
English Civil War.

Cross the field, heading away from the
road to the corner of the trees. Go into
Pepperboxes Wood, named after two

◀ Hampden House

lodges below Hampden House. Turn left at a bridleway, then climb a stile into the Glade. The trees in this avenue were felled in the 16th century when Queen Elizabeth visited Hampden because she was known to enjoy a view from her bedchamber.

Walk up the grass towards Hampden House to a road. Turn right and go downhill to a junction. The path resumes a few paces to the left on the other side of the road. It runs up a field, first with the hedge on your left, then with the hedge on your right as you follow the field edge up to Little Hampden Farm. Go left on a farm track, before turning left again at Warren Cottage. The path leads through woods to a marker post with arrows pointing both ways.

Head right to leave the woods and then left to walk round the edge of a field until a marker post directs you back through trees. At the next field, go right to follow the path down through a gate and into more woodland. Then turn left onto a path which leads downhill to a road.

Cross over and bear left up the slope and back into trees. Follow the path uphill to pass Hampden House on your left.

With a history dating back to before the Norman Conquest, it has latterly been used as a school, a wedding venue and as a production base for Hammer Films; the house appeared in many episodes of their low-budget TV series in the 1970s.

Turn left on the track, then go right to walk past the entrance to the church, where a path from the far side of the churchyard leads across pasture. Cross a farm road and the path leads you over a field to reach a track. A left turn will take you back to your start point at the Hampden Arms.

57

Chesham to Little Chalfont

Distance **8km** Time **2 hours 30 (one way)**
Terrain **footpaths and town pavements**
Maps **OS Explorer 172 and 181**
Access **Underground trains from London
and buses from Hemel Hempstead and
High Wycombe to Chesham;
Underground from Chalfont & Latimer
Station to return to the start**

**The market town of Chesham is literally
at the end of the line – the Metropolitan
Line from London. It means the London
Underground network is just a short
distance from the delightful Chess
Valley, allowing for a lovely walk
downstream to Latimer and across the
river to Little Chalfont.**

There are several pay and display car
parks in Chesham, or a free one in Moor
Road (HP5 1SE) which is just over 1km
from the station and on this route.

From the station, go immediately left
down steps and left again to walk beside

the railway. After 250m, turn right into
Punchbowl Lane. Cross the busy street
into Meades Water Garden, and follow the
path to a road beside a roundabout. Cross
Amersham Road and go into Moor Road,
following it until it goes left after the
swimming pool. Here, the route goes
straight ahead onto playing fields. Keep to
the left side to find the footpath as it
enters some woodland by a bench. It
follows the riverbank to a weir, the site of
a Saxon cornmill.

The path continues now with the river
on the right, until you turn right onto a
footbridge which will lead you through an
industrial estate to a field. Head left and
follow the stream to a track leading to
Holloway Lane. Walk carefully along the
narrow verge to a road junction. Cross the
busy road when it is safe to do so, then
turn left to pass the recycling centre and
go over a bridge. As the road swings left,
carry on over the wide lay-by onto a

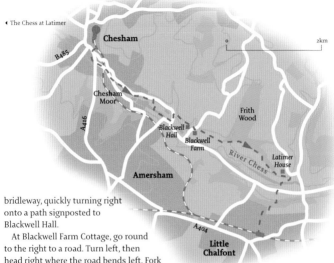

◄ The Chess at Latimer

bridleway, quickly turning right onto a path signposted to Blackwell Hall.

At Blackwell Farm Cottage, go round to the right to a road. Turn left, then head right where the road bends left. Fork right past the farm buildings, then right again to walk along the bottom of three fields to woodland. Where the path starts to climb, cross a stile to walk uphill with the trees to your left and the River Chess over to your right. Follow the field edge to a gate to continue inside a fence, looking over the Great Water where the river was dammed to create a lake.

The present Latimer House, on your left, dates from the 19th century after an Elizabethan manor was destroyed by fire. It was bombed by the IRA when it was the National Defence College in the 1970s and is now a hotel.

After passing the house, turn right onto a track dropping downhill to cross by a weir. Where the track forks, go through a gate and walk over the pasture. Cross the road and head up to the trees, with a fence at your left hand. Once in the woods, walk a few paces up from the gate to turn right onto a wide track which climbs uphill to the top of the woods.

You will emerge close to a house at the top, where a car park leads you out to Chenies Avenue. Turn left and, after 250m, go straight across Elizabeth Avenue and continue downhill to the junction. Turn left to reach Chalfont & Latimer Station. From here you can catch the Underground back to Chesham or, if you prefer, nip into London to catch a show!

Bledlow to Chinnor

Distance 6.25km **Time 2 hours 30**
Terrain paths and tracks
**Map OS Explorer 181 Access buses from
Chinnor & Princes Risborough to Bledlow**

Bledlow's church and pub will be familiar
to viewers of *Midsomer Murders*. They have
appeared in several episodes of the TV
detective series, with producers taking
advantage of their traditional English
appearance and quiet location. Chinnor
Cement Works also doubled for North
Korea during the hovercraft chase in the
Bond film *Die Another Day*. This walk is
not far off the beaten track but feels
remote and tranquil.

   There is plenty of parking on the village
street which links Bledlow's church and
its pub (HP27 9PE). With the pub on your
left, head out across the field, turning
right where it joins a track. After 400m,
climb the stile on your right to walk

across fields beside a fence. A stile lets
you into a paddock in front of Lower
Wainhill Farm, and a gate lets you out in
the right-hand corner by a timber shed.

   As you leave the farm, turn right on the
road before turning left where a sign
points to Chinnor after 25m. Follow the
narrow path until it opens out into fields
parallel to the Chinnor & Princes
Risborough Railway. If you are lucky, you
may see one of the steam trains making
the short journey between the towns. Its
whistle, which can be heard for miles, will
give you warning.

   At a T-junction, you can go right for
Chinnor, but to continue the walk turn
left up a path known as Keens Lane. Cross
the wide Ridgeway track at the top and
head on up the hill. Keep right at a fork
and before long you will find yourself
following a well-trodden path up the
fairly steep hillside. Near the top, the path

Bledlow

enters a deeper gully. Look for wooden steps leading up to the left – white arrows on the trees will guide you if necessary – and continue through woods to a road.

Turn left and walk to a car park. At the far end, a gate beside a horse-friendly barrier marks the start of the Chinnor Barrows bridleway. Some 400m after the information board, you come to a gate onto open ground to your left, where the views can be outstanding. When ready, go right, passing benches and into woodland. You will pass a noticeboard pointing out a small Chalk Pit nature reserve just on your left-hand side.

Soon after the bridleway and footpath separate, walkers are well advised to take the high road, just to the left of the deep gully as it runs down the hillside. Hidden in the trees up to your right is the Bledlow Cross, a 20m by 20m cross cut into the chalky hillside. Its origins are unknown and, of all the Chiltern chalk carvings, it is the least appreciated, probably because it is hidden by undergrowth and woodland.

The path comes out of the trees with a brick-built house at your right hand. At the crossroads of paths and tracks, go right for the Ridgeway & Icknield Way. This leads round the hillside, soon climbing gently. Where paths cross at the top, go left to return downhill to the pub in Bledlow.

Before you leave, it is worth visiting the church, largely unaltered since it was built in the 12th century. Beside the church, down steps, are the Lyde Gardens, created from disused watercress beds by Lord and Lady Carrington. The gardens are open during daylight hours and entry is free.

Chinnor & Princes Risborough Railway

Chinnor

Lower Wainhill Farm

Wain Hill

Bledlow Cross

The Ridgeway

Bledlow Great Wood

Chinnor Hill

0   1km

◀ Chinnor train

Whiteleaf Cross and Pulpit Hill

Distance 5.5km **Time** 2 hours 30
Terrain paths and woodland tracks
Map OS Explorer 181 **Access** buses to
Monks Risborough, 1.4km from the start;
height-restricted car park, although there
is some space to park at the roadside

It is said that the famous Whiteleaf
Cross was once a pagan phallic symbol,
converted to a cross by monks in the
Middle Ages, although no-one really
knows who created it or why. Beyond
doubt, however, is the awe-inspiring
view from the hilltop. This walk also
features leafy woodlands, a nature
reserve and some interesting snippets
of military history.

From the A4010 in Monks Risborough,
take Peters Lane (signed for Hampden and
Whiteleaf) and follow it to the top of the
steep hill to find a car park on the left
(HP27 0RP). Set off past the information
board and turn right into the woods. You
will pass remnants of training trenches

from the First World War, then a Neolithic
burial mound before emerging on
Whiteleaf Hill. The Cross is to your left. It
is at its best when seen from a greater
distance, but go left if you prefer a close
view and then bear right, past a bench on
the summit, to rejoin the path.

This leads downhill, increasingly
steeply, until it bends right to a road. Turn
left to walk down beside a golf course to a
cricket pavilion. Go right, anticlockwise
round the boundary, where a gap in the
hedge opens onto a golf fairway.

Taking care to check it is safe to cross,
walk over the fairway to a tall green pole
supporting protective netting. Behind it
you will find a narrow path leading down
to a road, close to the Plough at Cadsden,
the pub where former prime minister
David Cameron famously left his eight-
year-old daughter by mistake after a
Sunday lunch.

Go left to walk up to a road junction and
look for the footpath on the other side,

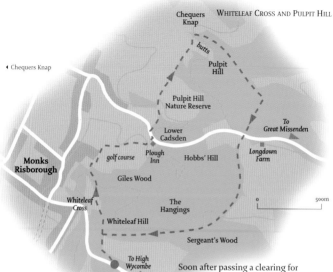

◄ Chequers Knap

Chequers
Knap

butts

Pulpit
Hill

Pulpit Hill
Nature Reserve

Lower
Cadsden

To
Great Missenden

golf course

Plough
Inn

Hobbs' Hill

Longdown
Farm

Monks
Risborough

Giles Wood

Whiteleaf
Cross

The
Hangings

Whiteleaf Hill

Sergeant's Wood

To High
Wycombe

0   500m

slighly to the left, which leads through woods to a choice of gates. Take the left gate to climb up a gentle slope. Cross a bridleway, then walk over the brow with woods to your right. Where the ground dips, the area to the right is the site of disused rifle butts, in use by the armed forces from the 1940s until the 1970s.

The path climbs to a gate into trees where it joins a sunken bridleway heading up the hillside. Turn uphill where, after a few paces, a gate lets you through to admire the view from Chequers Knap on your left. Return to follow the bridleway to the top of the hill. Don't be tempted by any paths which lure you away from the bridleway and, if in doubt, stick close to the boundary ditch beside you.

Soon after passing a clearing for electrical wires on your right, you come to a crossing of paths by a marker post where you turn right. Follow the path through the woods, across the same clearing for wires and then downhill to a road. Cross to a path by the entrance to Longdown Farm.

Walk with fields to your left, down to a dip where you cross an ancient holloway. Ignore the gate to your right and continue up the slope before bending right to join another path. A few paces further, turn left at a track to walk uphill until you see a track to your right, sealed off with a gate. To the left of the gate, a path leads along the hillside with the ground falling away to your right. Follow the path, maintaining height all the way, to reach the surfaced path on which you set out. A left turn leads back to the car park.

Chequers and Coombe Hill

Distance 7.5km **Time** 2 hours 30
Terrain paths and tracks, with a steep
descent near the start **Map** OS Explorer
181 **Access** buses from Aylesbury and
High Wycombe stop at Ellesborough
where you can pick up the walk

For almost a century, Chequers has been
the country retreat of Britain's prime
ministers, hosting royalty, presidents
and dignitaries in a manner befitting the
highest office in the land. So it is
remarkable that the public is allowed to
walk so close on a footpath that even
crosses the main drive. With some great
views, this is a glorious route.

From Butler's Cross, take Missenden
Road south for 1.5km, turning left to a
free car park at the top of Lodge Hill (HP17
0UR). Set off between two information
panels to follow a path across the heath.

Bear right after the gap in the trees to
reach the Boer War Memorial at Coombe
Hill, dedicated to the men of
Buckinghamshire who died in South
Africa between 1899 and 1902. At 260m
above sea level, it is the highest – and
perhaps the best – viewpoint in the
Chilterns. There is a topograph nearby to
make sense of the geography.

Head along the grassland, with the
ground falling away sharply to your right,
to join a path heading steeply downhill
with a fence on your left. It leads down
through trees to a track and on to
Missenden Road at the bottom. Cross over
and turn right. After 100m, take a footpath
on the left over a field. It enters a thicket
to join a track. Go right to reach the main
road opposite a church.

Turn left along the narrow path to a
gate just beyond the bus stop. The path

◄ Coombe Hill Boer War Memorial

now crosses the field towards the right-hand side of Beacon Hill. After passing through the gate in the hedge below the hill, you have a choice. If you're feeling energetic, climb straight to the summit; on a clear day the views make it well worth the effort. If you want to conserve your energy, take the path to the right of the hill. It leads to a gate into Ellesborough Warren, once a medieval rabbit farm, now one of only three surviving areas of native boxwood in the country.

The path leads up steps and across a field to a gate into woodland. Once through the woods, cross a track to a gate just beyond. You will start to see notices warning of the dangers of trespassing as you get close to Chequers; take care to stay on the right path or you could fall foul of the 2005 Serious Organised Crime & Police Act.

Walk up the left side of the field by the fence to the corner. Go right, along the edge of the woodland, with views over Chequers to your left. When the view is obscured by undergrowth, a sign directs you left on the Ridgeway, across open fields in front of Chequers, over the driveway and across another field to a road.

Cross over and take the path heading left by the entrance to Buckmoorend Farm. Follow the Ridgeway signs up the hill and through the woodland, ignoring any paths which head off on either side. Regular marker posts will keep you on the path as it bears left to eventually reach a road. On the other side, a few steps up to your right, take the path leading into the woods. It takes you through mature coppiced beeches, keeping a field visible through trees on your right. When you reach a gate, turn right for the short walk back to the car park.

Cholesbury

Distance 9.5km **Time** 3 hours 30
Terrain quiet lanes and woodland paths
Map OS Explorer 181 **Access** buses from
Chesham to Cholesbury Cricket Ground

You won't find many more impressive
Iron Age forts than the one at Cholesbury.
Known locally as the Camp, three-quarters
of the ditch and ramparts have survived,
encircling paddocks, a pond and the
parish church. This route can easily be
separated into two if preferred.

Cholesbury's cricket pitch sits on the
common by the road with a parking area
beside it (HP23 6ND). With your back to the
pavilion, head right to cross the road to
Wigginton and walk to the village hall.
A gate beside it leads into a paddock.

The circle of beech trees around you
denotes the extent of the ancient fort.
The small body of water – never known to

run dry – is called the Holy Pond. Take the
gate over to your left to pass the 900-year-
old St Laurence Church, and walk out onto
Parrott's Lane.

Cross to a short path, beginning to the
left of the entrance to Danesfield and
ending at a road. Turn right and, after 30m,
take the gate on the right which lets you
walk up through a field towards the top.
Ignore the first gate on the left and take
the second, some 30m further on. Keep to
the left of the field where a wooden gate
opens to a path beside a hedge. It leads to
Broomstick Lane where you walk up
between houses to a junction. Turn left
and go downhill into Buckland Common.

Bear right across the green onto Little
Twye Road, and follow it to Beechwood
Farm where a bridleway continues up the
edge of the woods. Where the field ends on
your right, turn right and wander down

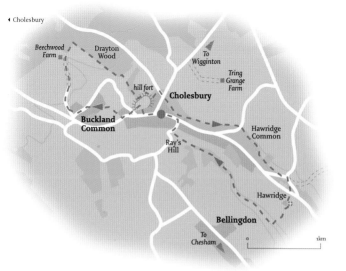

‹ Cholesbury

Beechwood Farm
Drayton Wood
To Wigginton
Tring Grange Farm
hill fort
Cholesbury
Buckland Common
Ray's Hill
Hawridge Common
Hawridge
Bellingdon
To Chesham
0   1km

through Drayton Wood, keeping close to the right-hand side. Ignore a stile in the fence and walk on along the path as it bends to the left. Go through a gate leading right along the edge of a field into Tomlins Wood. Keep right at a fork to meander through trees to the hillfort.

Turn left to walk for 250m between the ramparts, bending round to the right. When you see a house on the left across a paddock, take the path out to Shire Lane, leaving the house to your right. Go right to a T-junction. A right turn here will take you back to Cholesbury, but if you want to walk further then cross the road onto the common, following the path ahead until you are walking with fields to your left.

After 1km, cross Horseblock Lane by going left for a few metres onto a path along the edge of the woods. It leads to an unsurfaced road with houses on your left, then to a surfaced road and, 50m beyond, to a road junction. Walk round to the right where, just after the signpost, a footpath heads into trees, emerging onto a road.

Cross carefully and follow Church Lane to the end. Look for a narrow path between a beech hedge and the left-hand side of a brick house. This leads to a field. Walk down to the valley bottom and turn right. Follow the footpath along the valley, ignoring all other paths, to meet a tarmac lane at Ray's Hill. A right turn brings you up the road where the cricket pitch can be seen over to your left.

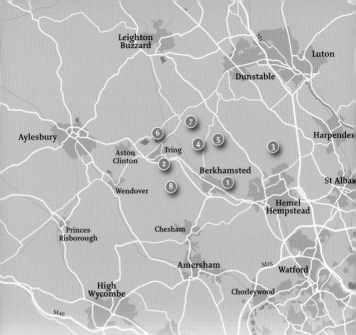

The towns of Tring and Berkhamsted sit in a small Hertfordshire isthmus, jutting impertinently into the eastern flank of Buckinghamshire. They are just a few miles apart on an old Roman road known as Akeman Street – near neighbours but with a very different history.

It was at Berkhamsted in 1066 that the English noblemen conceded defeat to William the Conquerer. William promptly gave the town to his half-brother who used the locals to build him a mighty castle. It was besieged by both English and French armies, and served as a home to kings and courtiers for more than four hundred years before being abandoned in 1495.

Tring, on the other hand, sitting peacefully at the crossroads of Akeman Street and the Icknield Way, was largely ignored by history until the very wealthy Rothschild family arrived in the 1870s and started investing in the town and its surroundings.

Between them is the Ashridge Estate, now owned by the National Trust. Although the house at its centre – favourite royal residence in Elizabethan times – has been replaced by a flamboyant Gothic pile, the fine parkland and estate are there to be enjoyed by king and commoner alike.

68

Dockey Wood, Ivinghoe ▲

Tring and Berkhamsted

Berkhamsted and the Alpine Meadow

Distance **6.5km** Time **2 hours**
Terrain **paths and muddy bridleways**
Map **OS Explorer 181** Access **buses from Chesham stop in Bridle Way, close to the start of the walk**

The Alpine Meadow is a little haven of peace, set in a quiet dell just north of Berkhamsted. It is rich in wildflowers, butterflies and birds. The perfect place for a picnic as you walk from the town out to the Ashridge Estate and back.

You should be able to park in Bridle Way, the road leading up to Bridgewater School on the north side of Berkhamsted (HP4 1ES). The path begins at the junction at the top of the hill, just where cars turn right for the school.

A footpath sign on a lamppost points the way into the trees and you will find yourself on a wide path which gently bears round to the right until you join a road. Go straight ahead, walking along the surfaced road which soon becomes unsurfaced with houses on your right. Follow it around to the left and up to the semicircle of grass at the entrance to Northchurch Farm.

Footpaths go off in all directions at this point, but your route lies on the far side of the grass, just left of the white access gates. Keep the hedge to your left and walk up past the buildings where the path sets off across the field. There is a marker post to help you find the direction across, aiming for another post on the far side. Turn left when you reach the far marker, then right to walk down between a hedge and a fence.

Go through the gate at the bottom and onto a farm track which leads you through a dip to another field. Go right to walk up the track with the hedge to your right. Follow the track for 800m to a gate into a paddock at Coldharbour Farm. Cross this towards the house and pass

◀ Near Berkhamsted

through the gates, turning right onto the wide path that starts a few paces later.

This is Berkhamsted Common which has remained commonland in spite of several attempts by the owners of Ashridge Estate to enclose it. The most famous was the Battle of Berkhamsted Common in 1866, when local campaigners recruited London 'muscle' to tear down the three miles of high iron fencing erected by the estate's owner. The land was never enclosed again and it was sold 60 years later to the National Trust.

Follow the track, going right when you come to a fork. After 350m, head right at the sign for the Alpine Meadow. Go through a gate at the edge of the woods to walk down the side of the fields to the Alpine Meadow Reserve. It's a lovely quiet glade, rich in wildflowers and butterflies from spring until autumn, birdsong fills the air and you might also spot a lizard or two on the log piles if you keep your eyes peeled.

Follow the path through the reserve and up the other side of the valley. For the next 1km keep close to the edge of the fields as you walk towards the town. Go through a gate in the corner of the field to shortly cross a path and a few moments later you will pass Bridgewater School on your left. The start point is a short distance away.

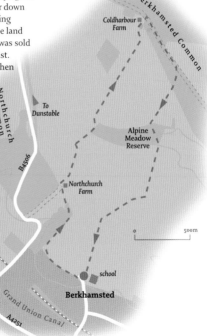

Tring Park to Wendover Woods

Distance 12km Time 4 hours
Terrain **paths, tracks and short sections
of quiet country lanes** Map **OS Explorer 181**
Access **buses from Aylesbury, Hemel
Hempstead and Watford to Tring; bus
from Tring Station stops in the High
Street, 450m from the start**

This corner of England was once known
as 'Rothschildshire' and the influence of
the famous banking family is clear to see,
not least in the Natural History Museum
close to the start. It's a great walk with a
handy refreshment stop in some of the
finest woods in England.

Park on the roadside in Hastoe Lane
close to the Natural History Museum
(HP23 6AP). With the museum to your
left, walk up Park Street for 90m to where
a footpath goes off right to a footbridge
over the A41 and into Tring Park.

The bridge provides a good view of an

avenue of trees, with the mansion – now
the Tring Park School for the Performing
Arts – at the northern end. At the bottom
of the steps, take the path to the left of the
information board and head to a marker
post, where you bear left, then right to
walk up to the trees. A gate opens onto a
track leading up to an 18th-century
obelisk, known as Nell Gwyn's
Monument, with a summerhouse beyond.

From the monument to King Charles II's
orange-selling mistress, take the path
heading right up the slope until it merges
with a track called King Charles Ride. Turn
right along what is now also part of the
Ridgeway Trail and follow it through the
woods, eventually bending to the left and
emerging onto a public road. Turn left to
a road junction, then right into Church
Lane to reach a crossroads in Hastoe.

Continue straight along Gadmore Lane
(signed Ridgeway), until the road bends

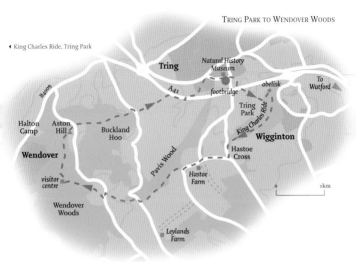

◀ King Charles Ride, Tring Park

sharp left. Now plunge into the woods and follow the path until it emerges onto a road by a communications mast. The Ridgeway goes left, but this route continues straight over (signed Icknield Way). Follow the edge of the woods with gardens to your left to walk above a valley towards a house with impressive oak-framed extensions.

Head left on the road for 100m to a footpath across a field on the right leading into woods. Once in the trees, the path can be hard to discern, but bear left if in doubt and you will emerge on a tarmac exit road from the Wendover Wood Visitor Centre. Turn right and, when the road bears left to the visitor centre car park, leave it to walk straight ahead over an unsurfaced parking area and a strip of grass and out onto the visitor centre's tarmac entry road.

Go right for 250m to a path on the right,

heading past a vehicle barrier. As you approach a gate blocking your way, a path leads right, past the Aston Hill trig point, to a road. Drop downhill for a few steps before turning right onto a Forestry Commission track. A path takes up where the track ends, leading down through the woods to a road. Walk right for 50m, then left onto a narrow path which soon opens onto a pleasant stretch down the edge of fields, crossing other paths until you turn right beside the A41.

When you reach Duckmore Lane via a concrete ramp, turn left under the bypass, then immediately right over a meadow to a kissing gate. The path now leads down behind gardens to Park Road – the line of the old Roman Akeman Street – and a right turn will take you back to Hastoe Lane with the Natural History Museum just beyond.

From Gaddesden Row

Distance **9.5km** Time **3 hours**
Terrain **paths, fields and bridleways**
Map **OS Explorer 182** Access **buses from Hemel Hempstead and Luton to Gaddesden Row**

It may be Jockey End on the map but the locals – and roadsigns – call it Gaddesden Row. The Jockey was a pub which burnt down more than a hundred years ago, and the mapmakers have apparently never got over it. This walk passes through parkland designed by the greatest landscape designer in English history.

From the green in Gaddesden Row (or 'Jockey End' if you prefer) head down out of the village on Bradden Lane, opposite the Methodist church (HP2 6HR). After 500m, turn left onto a track to Bunkers House. Step left at the gateway to walk beside the garden to a field, and turn right. Go past the hedge on your right and across the field, aiming for a gap in the far hedge. Turn left on a footpath to a gate opening right, into a field, after 200m.

The house ahead is called The Hoo. It is the birthplace of at least 1270 babies, mostly from its days as a maternity hospital during the Second World War. The parkland was originally laid out by Capability Brown. When you reach the fence by the garden, bear right beside a fence to Hoo Wood. The path descends to a gate beside an oak bench and across a field. If the path is hard to see, walk in a straight line as if you have just risen from the bench.

At the far side, bear right to a road. Cross to the field opposite where a footbridge goes over wet ground, before heading left towards the church in Great Gaddesden. Keep the houses and school to your right as you walk to a road junction. Just uphill, a footpath begins by the entrance to Sybden House. Keep roughly to the right-hand side of the field

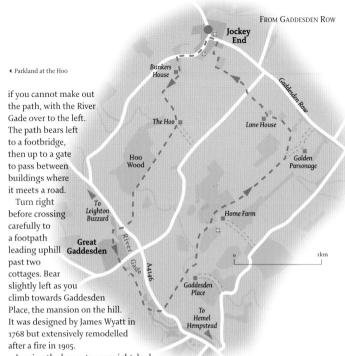

◂ Parkland at the Hoo

if you cannot make out the path, with the River Gade over to the left. The path bears left to a footbridge, then up to a gate to pass between buildings where it meets a road.

Turn right before crossing carefully to a footpath leading uphill past two cottages. Bear slightly left as you climb towards Gaddesden Place, the mansion on the hill. It was designed by James Wyatt in 1768 but extensively remodelled after a fire in 1905.

Leaving the house to your right, look for the gate in the fence by a marker post, then turn left to follow the fence down to another gate. The path then continues up the slope, bending right into woodland. Cross a track to walk past farm buildings. At a farm track, go left and walk towards the Golden Parsonage. The Halsey family has lived here since 1520, although the classical red-brick house standing today dates from the 18th century.

Near the house, the path passes between posts by a waymarked gate. Bear left over a meadow and go through two gates. Turn left along the edge of a field, and left again onto the drive to the Lane House, walking round the pond on your right to a gate. Cross the fields to a lane. Go right for a few metres to rejoin the path as it runs between paddocks past Six Tunnels Farm.

Carry on in the same direction, ignoring any gates to your right, until you come to a yellow marker post at the corner of a hedge. Turn right and follow the hedge, round a left and right bend, back to Gaddesden Row.

Bridgewater Monument to the Pitstone Windmill

Distance **10km** Time **3 hours**
Terrain **paths and a stretch of minor road**
Map **OS Explorer 181** Access **buses from Hemel Hempstead and Berkhamsted stop at Monument Drive, a 10-minute walk from the start**

A bracing hike from an iconic monument to England's oldest windmill. The Ashridge Estate is one of the National Trust's treasures, enjoyable at any time of the year with splendid trees and views.

The visitor centre sits beside a tall granite column erected in memory of the Third Duke of Bridgewater (HP4 1LX). He built what many regard as the first canal in England and is known as 'the father of British inland navigation'. From the visitor centre, pass the monument on the right-hand path, marked 'Mobility Trail'.

This sets off into woods along the edge of a ridge. After roughly 2km, just past a house on the right, go through a gate and turn left onto a track. Take a footpath on the left after 200m and follow it downhill and out of the woods until you are crossing grassland, with a fence on your left.

At a crossing of paths (where there is a sign warning against touching any old munitions) go straight on. It is signed to Ivinghoe, though the path is less defined as it leads through a gate, across a field and alongside a hedge. This section allows some delightful views of Ivinghoe Beacon through the hedge to your right.

A gate in the corner opens onto a narrow path to the B488. Turn left without crossing the road – it is busy and the traffic moves quite fast – to walk up the narrow verge and cross, when safe, to the small car park on the bend. The windmill stands in the field ahead. The date, 1627, is carved into the woodwork,

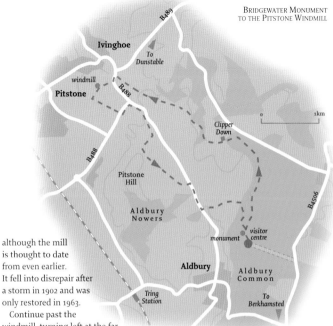

although the mill
is thought to date
from even earlier.
It fell into disrepair after
a storm in 1902 and was
only restored in 1963.

Continue past the
windmill, turning left at the far
side of the field to skirt along the
edge to a road. Cross both the road and
the wide grass verge through a gap in the
thicket. Turn left and follow the path
beside the road before it bends right and
narrows, now leading uphill to a field.
Walk over the grass until you see a path
which links a small parking area to your
left with Pitstone Hill to your right.

Ignore the path to the summit and take
the left fork to walk across the shoulder of
the hill, past an impressive holloway 'deep
enough to hide a man on his horse', to a
fence on the far side of the hill. Turn right
to follow the fence to its end where a gate

leads left onto a path along the field edge.

After 100m take the path heading across
the fields. When you are walking with a
rough hedge at your right hand, follow
the field margin to a road. Turn right. As
you approach a flint garden wall, a sign
directs you left to the Bridgewater
Monument. It leads past a stableyard and
onto a track up through the farmland to a
fork just below the treeline. Take the path
to the right which climbs up through the
woodland. At the next fork, go left to the
top of the hill, turning right onto a track
which leads back to the monument.

The Golden Valley and Prince's Riding

Distance **6km** Time **2 hours**
Terrain **grassland paths and wooded
tracks** Map OS Explorer **181** Access **buses
from Berkhamsted and Hemel
Hempstead stop at the road junction by
the start of the walk**

**The Ashridge Estate, now in the care of
the National Trust, boasts ancient
woodlands, carpets of bluebells in May,
outstanding views and plenty of deer and
other wildlife. This walk crosses a
famous valley created by Capability
Brown and an avenue of trees he was
forbidden to touch!**

There is a parking area close to the
junction of Hudnall Lane and the
Nettleden Road in Little Gaddesden (HP4
1PL). Take the path, opposite the entrance,
down the hill and into the trees to follow
a metal fence to a track. Turn left and walk
along the hillside to cross a little bridge,
ignoring a path down to a kissing gate.

Continue along the track until you can
head downhill on a slightly sunken path

between low walls. This leads down into
the Golden Valley. The view to the right,
up the gently undulating grassland
bounded by trees, was created by
Capability Brown. Three hundred years
ago, Brown had the ground here sculpted
and cleared and then re-planted to get the
valley looking just the way he wanted.
It is regarded as one of his masterpieces.

The path descends the valley side at an
angle, then heads up the other side,
leaving an oak bench to your left.
Ashridge House, which will appear
through the trees, has a history stretching
back some 800 years, first as a monastery,
then as an ostentatious family home to
the Earls of Bridgewater. It served as a
hospital in wartime and has been a
business school since 1958.

Cross in front of the house to walk
along the road until it bears left. Take the
track heading to the right, blocked by a
barrier, and follow it through the trees. It
leads to a road by the distinctive
chequered stonework of Thunderdell

◀ Ashridge House

Lodge. Cross with care, then turn right to walk along the verge to the entrance of the National Trust's Ashridge Estate Visitor Centre.

You are now at the Prince's Riding, an avenue of trees dating from just after the Civil War. It frames the view of the Bridgewater Monument from Ashridge House. Capability Brown hated straight lines and wanted to 'rearrange' the woodland here, but was told to leave it well alone!

Unless you plan to visit the monument erected in honour of the Third Duke of Bridgewater on this walk, go back across the road, round the wooden fence and follow the Prince's Riding towards the house. Just before a metal fence, the path goes right to avoid the golf green, then

bends round to the left, with the house over to your right.

Walk straight ahead into the copse. It doesn't look like much as you approach, but it includes some spectacular sweet chestnut trees, old enough to have survived Capability Brown's woodcutters, with their tortured and twisted trunks spiralling upwards. The path leads over the grass beyond the copse. Bear left to keep the next treeline on your right-hand side and walk down the slope.

Cross the road and head right, along the floor of the Golden Valley. After 350m, bear left to a gate leading to a stone bridge in the trees. At the bridge go left and walk back along the path to the metal fence. Turn right back up the slope and to the start of the walk.

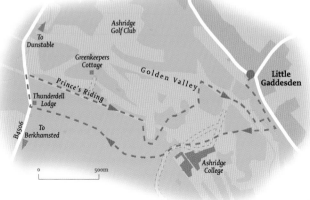

Tring's reservoirs and canals

Distance 7.5km **Time** 2 hours
Terrain canal towpaths, with some paths
and fields **Map** OS Explorer 181
Access buses from Hemel Hempstead,
Aylesbury and Dunstable stop close to
the car park at Startop's End

**The four reservoirs near Tring were built
more than two hundred years ago to
supply water to the Grand Union Canal.
While still serving that purpose today,
the reservoirs are also nature reserves
and well used by fishermen, birdwatchers
and walkers alike. And, now and again,
it's good to follow a route without any
steep climbs or descents!**

There is a small charge for parking at
Startop's End, but the money raised helps
maintain the canals, so you are supporting
a good cause. The car park is off the B489,
just north of Tring, beside the Bluebells
Tearoom (HP23 4LJ).

Walk to the far end of the car park to join
the towpath, with the Grand Union Canal
to your left as it rises very gently up
through a flight of locks. Built around 1800,
the canal links London to Birmingham.

At the Top Lock the towpath crosses a
bridge over the Wendover Arm of the
canal. Turn sharp left once over the
bridge to walk under it, so that you are
now walking with the Wendover Arm by
your right hand. This canal was built to
feed water into the main system, but it
leaked so badly that it was closed in
1904 and large parts of it were drained.
Work is currently underway to restore
the canal to allow boats to reach
Wendover for the first time in more
than a century.

Follow the towpath for 1km to a bridge
where you cross – with care – to the other
side to rejoin the towpath, now with the
canal on your left. After passing Heygates
Flour Mill, look out for the turning point
on the far bank at the end of a long canal-

◄ Grand Union Canal

side garden. This used to mark the limit of navigable water.

At the next bridge, leave the towpath to cross the bridge. Take a path going right, signposted to Wilstone Reservoir. After 150m, the path bears away from the canal, then turns right after passing through a gate. Walk up the edge of the field to be reunited with the Wendover Arm, this part of it under restoration.

After crossing the canal, go right for a few steps to a path heading left. Turn right where the path joins a track and then turn left after 200m to walk beside Wilstone Reservoir. Two-thirds of the way along, take the steps down the embankment on your right, go through the two gates and, keeping left at a fork, walk down to a road.

Cross into Wilstone, and walk up the verge to a gate leading right, just after New Road. Cut slightly left across a field, before turning left into New Road to walk down to the war memorial. Go right into Rosebarn Lane, continuing ahead where it becomes a path, with allotments to your left. Go through a gap in the hedge to cross a field to the Aylesbury Arm of the Grand Union. Turn right and follow the towpath for 1.25km until you see the Bluebells Tearoom on your right. You can reward yourself with a cup of tea or an ice-cream before heading home.

Ivinghoe Beacon

Distance **8km** Time **2 hours 30**
Terrain **paths and tracks**
Map **OS Explorer 181** Access **no public transport to the start**

The bluebell woods of the Chilterns are arguably the finest in the country if you pick the right time to visit. Nowhere is this better exemplified than in Dockey Wood immediately opposite the start of this walk. On this route, you will be rewarded with beech trees, chalk grasslands and views from the top of the escarpment. Quintessentially Chiltern!

The National Trust provides free parking opposite Dockey Wood (HP4 1NF). It is reached by turning off the B489 at the brown sign to Ivinghoe Beacon, and driving south for 3.5km. If your visit coincides with the bluebell season, cross the road to wander through the woods before returning to the car park.

Head left along the road for 250m to a footpath on your right-hand side. This leads diagonally left across two fields, aiming for the left side of Ward's Hurst Farm. Turn right on the farm track, then left and right to pass between the buildings. In the distance ahead, you should be able to see the Whipsnade Lion carved into the chalk hillside on Dunstable Downs.

Go left into woods, keeping to the right to descend wooden steps. At the bottom, branch left after 200m, crossing a corridor of conifers to follow the path through more fir trees. When you emerge, go over a track into more open woodland to a gate opening into a field. Aim for the marker post on the brow, bearing right to join a path leading across the field to the left end of a line of trees 500m away.

With the high ridge of Ivinghoe Beacon to your left and trees to your right, keep

◀ Waymarker, Ivinghoe

to the edge of the fields before turning left and heading up Gallows Hill. You pass a burial mound close to the top. The path to Ivinghoe Beacon runs along the ridge, bearing west.

The trig point is 233m above sea level and, while the view is not completely panoramic, on a clear day it is certainly spectacular. To the east is Whipsnade, easily spotted because of the lion. Looking to the southwest, you should be able to see the Pitstone Windmill – England's oldest – as well as the peaceful Tring Reservoirs.

With your back to the writing on the plinth by the trig point, walk straight ahead, taking you south over the downs to cross a road by a barrier and up the hill on the other side. Keep to the wider track which heads uphill, forking right near the brow. Follow it through the low woodland until it turns downhill beside the steep-sided Inchcombe Hole, often used for endurance training for people planning to trek the Himalayas. You can see the footsteps up the far side – as exhausting a climb as you'll find in the Chiltern Hills.

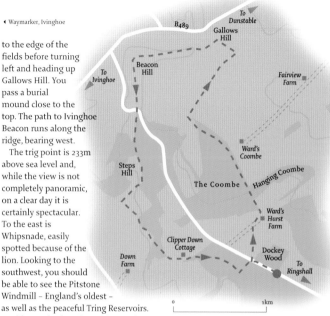

Where paths cross at the corner of a field, turn left to walk gently uphill, keeping left at the fork before going into woodland. Bear right onto a track which will lead you past Clipper Down Cottage. Around 400m further along, take the path heading left. This will lead you back to the public road with your car parked along to the right. If you prefer not to walk on the road, it is easy to pick your way through the woods beside it until you reach the car park.

83

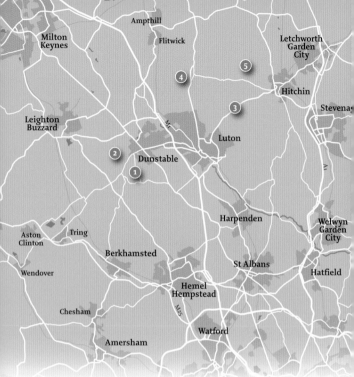

Many people – and a good few guidebooks – seem to think the Chilterns stop at Dunstable and Luton. Yet those two towns, sitting astride the M1 motorway, are simply a short urban intermission in the Chilterns Area of Outstanding Natural Beauty.

The landscape along the Bedfordshire and Hertfordshire border, to the west of Hitchin, is recognisably Chiltern with wooded hills and valleys and a hint of the downland so familiar further south.

John Bunyan walked this countryside as a tinker before he wrote *Pilgrim's Progress*, and is believed to have modelled the Delectable Mountains on Sharpenhoe's Sundon Hills.

This part of the Chilterns is explored by fewer people than the hotspots in Oxfordshire and Buckinghamshire. Dunstable Downs, on the other hand, which stretch south to Whipsnade (of zoo fame), can be busy on a bright summer's day, but it only takes a couple of minutes' walk to be clear of the crowds.

The North

Dunstable Downs and Whipsnade

Distance **7km** Time **2 hours 30**
Terrain **path and bridleways**
Map **OS Explorer 182** Access **buses from
Luton to Whipsnade to pick up the walk
from the Tree Cathedral**

**Dunstable Downs can be a busy place with
holidaymakers, walkers, kite flyers and
hang- gliders all competing for space. But
it doesn't take long to leave them behind
for this delightful outing along the ridge
to Whipsnade Tree Cathedral and onto
Whipsnade Heath.**

Park at the Chilterns Gateway Centre
where there's a modest daily charge
(LU6 2GY). When conditions are right,
hang-gliders launch themselves into the
air from the top of the ridge and gliders
are hauled into the sky by aircraft from
the airfield below. It makes for a
spectacular, if busy, location to soak
up the action.

On the edge of the ridge is a metal
sculpture called the *Windcatcher* which
draws air from the hillside to ventilate the
visitor centre 90m behind it. With the
Windcatcher in front of you and the centre
behind, go left along the ridge. Ignore the
path to the Tree Cathedral which tempts
you left, but continue to walk along the
downs with a good view of Ivinghoe
Beacon ahead.

When the path bends slowly left to
overlook a car park on the right, turn left
onto a bridleway flanked by hedges. After
500m, pass between high wooden fences,
then take the path heading left. It leads
beside a field to the Whipsnade Tree
Cathedral. This was a simple hayfield
until Edmund Blyth began planting trees
in memory of his comrades-in-arms who
died in the First World War. The trees form
the walls of the cloisters, transepts, nave
and chancel.

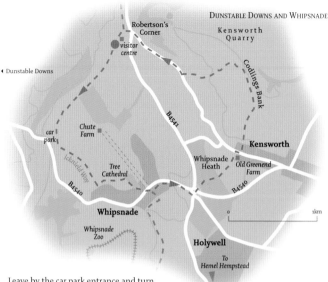

◀ Dunstable Downs

Leave by the car park entrance and turn left in front of houses to the road. Cross with care and walk down the wide village green to the road by the thatched pub, the Old Hunters Lodge. Don't cross the road but take the wooded path beside it, emerging to the right of a roundabout.

Cross the road ahead of you, then go left and cross the next road (effectively bypassing the roundabout). Ahead is the entrance to Whipsnade Heath and a path which leads up through woodland. Continue to follow the edge of a field, then over pasture to a quiet public road by Old Greenend Farm.

Go right for 50m, then cross the road to enter a path which, for the first 100m, feels squeezed between commercial buildings. It soon opens out to overlook a wide dry valley. Head down the track to

leave the old tin shed on your left, turning left at a break in the hedge. The path now leads diagonally to Codlings Bank where you will pass a redundant kissing gate, then walk with a thicket on the bank to your right.

A gate at the far end opens onto a path where you should bear left downhill to pass a brick shed. When the path starts to rise, step right to walk up the side of a field with the hedge to your left, aiming for a communications mast among the trees. Follow the path left through the wood and out to a lane.

Go right and walk past the entrance to a quarry to the main road at Robertson's Corner. This is a fast stretch of road, so take great care in crossing back to the visitor centre.

Totternhoe Knolls

Distance **6.5km** Time **2 hours**
Terrain **tracks and paths**
Maps **OS Explorer 192 and 193**
Access **buses from Dunstable to Totternhoe**

Mankind has taken stone from Totternhoe
for more than two thousand years,
dramatically changing the landscape in the
process. Spoilheaps from ancient quarrying
formed the knolls after which the area is
named and it is now designated as a nature
reserve. This route runs over and around
the stone-workings, links two ancient forts
and follows a disused railway line.

A brown sign points to the car park just
off Castle Hill Road in Totternhoe (LU6
1RG). At the top of the steps from the
parking area, go right for a few paces to a
track, then turn left. As you walk, look
across the flat field to the right. A hill here
was entirely removed for its stone and
lime content in the 1980s.

Totternhoe stone – or 'clunch' – is soft

and easy to work, but weathers quickly
when used outside. It has always been
prized for interior decoration in some of
the country's finest buildings, including
Westminster Abbey, Windsor Castle and
Woburn Abbey.

Follow the path as it climbs gently.
Where it turns to the right, leave it for a
gate on the left to join a path which passes
three defensive ditches (or 'baileys') to
Castle Hill. This earth mound (or 'motte')
was the site of an 11th-century castle
which the Normans called *Eglemunt* –
'Eagle Mount'. There is a glorious view
from the top.

Go through the gate on the other side of
the mound for a fine view of the medieval
quarrying after which the area is named.
Bear right down the hillside to a gate and
then left on the path downhill.

Near the bottom, take a path which cuts
back to the right, waymarked by a yellow
post. It leads along the edges of fields,

◀ Castle Hill, Totternhoe

with several turns, to meet a road. Turn right, past a barrier, to reach a crossroads.

Turn left and, after 250m, go right onto the Sewell Greenway. Follow this old railway line for 1.5km, keeping an eye out for the ruins of a platform down to the right. From here the quarried stone was hauled up the embankment on ropes to be taken away by train. As the path crosses a timber bridge and approaches a deep cutting, take a path to the right down the embankment to a track. Turn left and walk up the incline for 130m where a path goes right, onto the grass.

Go round the clump of trees on your right into the Maiden Bower, a huge circle of trees delineating an Iron Age fort. Turn left and walk round the circle for 100m where a gap lets you step through into a narrow section of a field. Go through the hedge ahead, then turn right. Follow the track as it bends right to a crossroads by an ornate wooden bench.

Turn right to walk between hedges for 700m to a junction of tracks. Turn left, past chalk cliffs to your right, then turn right on a path leading over the rise behind the cliff. The view to your right gives you an idea of just how much stone has been removed! At the bottom of the slope, go left at the crossroads, then left again to the car park steps.

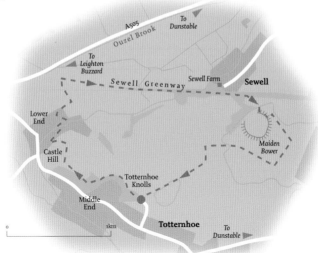

Lilley to Telegraph Hill

Distance **7km** Time **2 hours 30**
Terrain **fields and tracks**
Map **OS Explorer 193** Access **buses from
Stevenage and Luton to West Street,
Lilley, 350m from the start**

During the Napoleonic Wars, Telegraph
Hill had a vital role in the country's
defences. A wooden hut, 183m above sea
level, was one link in a chain from Great
Yarmouth to London to give early
warning of the arrival of foreign forces.
The hut is long gone, but the hill remains
as a focal point for this invigorating walk
into the Hertfordshire countryside.

Lilley is just off the A505 between Luton
and Hitchin. Roadside parking is available
on West Street, near the Lilley Arms (LU2
8LN). Set off with the pub to your right
and walk to the main road, crossing in
front of Church Farm.

Head left for 180m to take the first track
on the right, a bridleway called the Baulk.
It leads down past a house to a crossing of
paths. Go left (signed John Bunyan Trail)
to walk along the edge of the fields. As
you continue along the valley bottom,
ignore Kingshill Lane which leads uphill
to your right between hedges, and carry on
along the field edges to join a farm track;
follow it left and then right until you meet
a track running from left to right.

This is the Icknield Way, part of the
original route along which people have
travelled for thousands of years. Turn
right to walk up between hedges and then
trees. When you reach a fork, bear left.

Soon you will notice you are next to a
holloway with others further to the right.
As our forebears walked, rode, or drove
animals up the hillside, the ground would
become muddy and impassable. When

Pegsdon Hills
Nature Reserve

Hoo Bit

Telegraph
Hill

0   1km

The Icknield Way

Lilley Hoo

Kingshill Lane

Lilley Hoo
Farm

Lilleyhoo Lane

Lilley

A505

To
Luton

needs demanded, they'd take another route nearby, alternating between paths according to the conditions. Each pathway has slowly been eroded underfoot over the millennia, creating the parallel gullies up the hillside that can still be seen today.

The path levels out near the site of the early 19th-century Lilley Hoo telegraph station. It worked by signalling, with a combination of open and closed shutters, along a chain stretching from the coast to the Admiralty in London. The system was scrapped in 1814, but this summit has been called Telegraph Hill ever since.

Keep to the path as it begins to go gently downhill, through the woodland, with the Pegsdon Hills and Hoo Bit Nature Reserve to your left. Go right where the paths meet, leaving the Icknield Way to pass through some woodland and into a field. This is Lilley Hoo, a grazing common until food shortages in the Second World War saw it ploughed and cultivated. Earlier, in the 17th and 18th centuries, these fields were the site of a racecourse, with George IV among those who came for the meetings.

The path heads straight across the field, aiming for a point between two electricity pylons. At a farm track, walk with the hedge on your right. Ignore a path to your right as you pass under the wires, continuing for another 50m to a footpath aiming diagonally off to the right with a low set marker post to indicate the start. At the far side, keep to the field margins with the woods at your right hand to reach a gate in the corner. Follow the path downhill and across the valley floor to rejoin the Baulk, at the top of which a left turn takes you back to the start.

Sharpenhoe Clappers

Distance 7km **Time** 2 hours
Terrain woodland paths and meadows, a
steep descent and an invigorating climb
Map OS Explorer 193 **Access** buses from
Luton stop at Streatley, 1km from the start

Sharpenhoe Clappers is a classic Chilterns
escarpment with chalk downland, beech
woodlands and superb views. It gets its
name from the Latin for rabbit warren
(*claperius*) – rabbits were farmed here for
more than a thousand years. Today it is
managed by the National Trust.

Streatley is easily found by travelling
north on the A6 and turning left 1.4km
after leaving Luton (LU3 3PN). From the
village follow signs to Sharpenhoe
Clappers car park, where parking is free.

A path leads from the parking area into
the woods. Keep right at the fork and, as
the path bends to the left, ignore the first
path to your right to take the second a few
paces later. This leads over the brow onto
sheep pasture. Turn left, keeping above the

young plantation, and enter the woods.
Ahead is a line of trees on a bank. Go
between the trees and turn right to follow
the path round the shoulder of the hill,
with the ground falling away to your right.

To your left are the remains of
earthworks, shown on the map as an Iron
Age fort, though recent archaeological
investigations suggest that there is no
evidence that the hill was ever fortified.
There is plenty of evidence, however, of
the hill's occupation by rabbits. For
several centuries they were farmed here
for food and fur.

Where the undergrowth thins out among
more mature beech trees, look down to
your right for a yellow marker at the top of
some wooden steps, around 70 in all, which
lead down the hillside. At the bottom, take
the footpath heading sharp left after the
National Trust sign to skirt round the foot
of the slope with the hill on your left. Go
through two gates and walk diagonally left
over the grass to a gate.

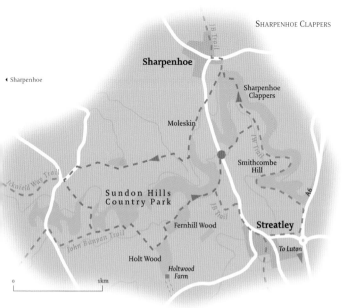

◀ Sharpenhoe

Sharpenhoe

Sharpenhoe Clappers

Moleskin

Smithcombe Hill

Sundon Hills Country Park

Fernhill Wood

Streatley

Holt Wood

Holtwood Farm

To Luton

0   1km

Cross the road onto a path which leads you round the foot of the hill, ignore the gate to Moleskin Hill on your left and continue until you reach the corner of the field. Turn right to walk along the narrow end of the field, then right again to head back up the other side. After about 100m, go left onto a track that runs between fields, past a small area of woodland and out to join the public road.

Go left for 250m along a wide verge to a road junction. Here the path runs left, gently uphill, between fields and into trees. Keep left in the woods to climb a flight of steps to a disused chalk quarry. At the top of the quarry, bear right to a gate in the top corner of the pasture. Follow the trees round and up the hillside,

then make for the left corner of the pasture where a clear path heads right.

From here until the end of the walk, your route is part of both the Icknield Way and John Bunyan Trails. After a quick left and right, the path crosses between fields to the corner of woodland. Turn left and then keep the woods to your right as you pass first Holt Wood and then, after a short stretch of open ground, Fernhill Wood. The path will eventually dive into the trees where you should bear right to walk along the top of the woodland – with the ground sloping away to your left – to reach a gate. Cross the pasture, making for a gate in the opposite fence. The car park is just across the road.

Pirton

Distance 6km **Time** 2 hours
Terrain bridleways, paths and fields
Map OS Explorer 193 **Access** buses from
Hitchin stop on Great Green, Pirton,
outside the pub

Pirton is as far north as this guidebook
takes you, and as far east as well. It may
be outside the designated Area of
Outstanding Natural Beauty (AONB), but
it is delightful countryside nonetheless.
Enjoy the ancient lanes, rolling hills and
historic buildings in this less travelled
corner of the Chilterns.

Park on the village green, opposite the
Motte and Bailey Pub (SG5 3QD). With the
green to your right, walk down the road to
a T-junction. The footpath begins directly
opposite, between the entrance to Pirton
Court and an electricity substation.

For the next 1.5km, follow the path as it
gently climbs uphill, with views over
farmland to the east, until it ends where
the path forks at the corner of a field.
Some 100m to your right is the entrance
to the Knocking Hoe National Nature
Reserve – a pleasant detour on a fine day.

This route takes the left path, along the
side of the field with a hedge on the left.
It leads to a gap in a hedge onto a busy
road. Traffic comes from both directions
at alarming speeds, so it is advisable to
walk a few steps to the right to improve
your sightlines before crossing.

Head up the road opposite. Ignore the
path on your left after 200m and continue,
past a metal gate with unusual traffic
lights, over the brow of the hill. Just
before a T-junction, take the footpath into
trees to your left by a marker post. Go
through an equestrian centre and then
straight ahead along a gravel track that
becomes a grassy path. The path bends
left, then right to take you round a pond
hidden in the undergrowth.